HOW TO START A GUN SHOP BUSINESS

The Ultimate Guide to Starting and Growing a Successful Firearm Dealership in a Competitive Market

Jeanelle K. Douglas

Copyright © 2024 by Jeanelle K. Douglas. All rights reserved. No part of this book, HOW TO START A GUN SHOP BUSINESS, may be reproduced, stored in a retrieval system, or transmitted in any form or by any means, electronic, mechanical, photocopying, recording, or otherwise, without the prior written permission of the author, Jeanelle K. Douglas.

Contents

INTRODUCTION 7

    Understanding the Firearms Industry 8

    Historical Context and Evolution of Gun 11

    Purpose and Scope of This Book 13

    Understanding the Different Types of Guns, Ammunition, and Accessories: 15

    The Importance of Responsible Gun Ownership 18

Role of Gun Stores in Promoting Safety and Education 21

    How to Handle and Store Gun in a Responsible Way 24

    Understanding Regulations and Legal Requirements 27

    Federal Laws and Regulations 29

    Overview of Federal Firearms License (FFL) 32

    Compliance with ATF Regulations 34

    Navigating the National Firearms Act (NFA) 37

    State Laws and Regulations 39

    Researching State-Specific Requirements 41

Licensing and Permits 44

    Compliance with Local Ordinances 46

    Market Research and Business Planning 48

- Identifying Target Market 51
  - Analyzing Competitors 54
- Creating a Business Plan 57
  - Market Analysis 64
- Organization and Management Structure 67
  - Marketing and Sales Strategies 69
  - Financial Projections 72
- Location Selection and Store Layout 75
  - Factors to Consider When Choosing a Location 77
  - Evaluating Demographics and Traffic Patterns 81
  - Designing an Effective Store Layout 83
  - Securing the Right Space and Negotiating Lease Terms 86
- Setting up Supplier Relationships 89
  - Identifying Reliable Suppliers 92
  - Establishing Vendor Relationships 95
  - Negotiating Terms and Pricing 98
  - Developing a Inventory Management Strategy 101
- Store Operations and Security 106
  - Hiring and Training Staff 111
  - Implementing Inventory Management Systems 115

    Ensuring Compliance with Security Measures 119

    Managing Day-to-Day Operations 123

Marketing and Promotions 127

    Developing a Marketing Plan 130

    Creating a Strong Brand Identity 134

    Utilizing Digital Marketing Channels 138

    Leveraging Traditional Advertising Methods 142

Hosting Events and Promotions 147

    Customer Service and Community Engagement 151

    Building Relationships with Customers 156

    Handling Customer Concerns and Feedback 158

Financial Management and Compliance 161

    Budgeting and Forecasting 164

    Tax Considerations for Gun Stores 167

    Ensuring Regulatory Compliance 170

Future Growth and Expansion 175

    Assessing Opportunities for Growth 179

    Expanding Product Offerings 182

    Scaling Operations 186

    Planning for Long-Term Success 189

Conclusion 193

Final Words of Advice 198

INTRODUCTION

A gun store, also known as a firearm or gun shop, is a retail establishment specializing in the sale of firearms, ammunition, accessories, and related equipment. These stores cater to a diverse customer base, including law enforcement agencies, shooting enthusiasts, hunters, collectors, and individuals seeking personal protection.

Gun stores play a crucial role in the firearms industry by providing a centralized location for purchasing firearms legally and responsibly. They are regulated by federal, state, and local laws to ensure compliance with firearm sales regulations and promote safety within communities.

In addition to retail sales, many gun stores offer services such as firearm transfers, gunsmithing, shooting range facilities, and educational courses on firearm safety and proficiency. These establishments serve as hubs for firearm enthusiasts to gather, exchange knowledge, and participate in various shooting activities.

Opening and operating a gun store requires a comprehensive understanding of firearms laws and regulations, as well as a commitment to promoting responsible firearm ownership. This book aims to provide aspiring entrepreneurs with practical guidance on navigating the legal landscape, conducting market research, establishing supplier relationships, managing operations, and building a successful gun store business.

Understanding the Firearms Industry

The firearms industry is a multifaceted sector that encompasses the manufacturing, distribution, sale, and use of firearms, ammunition, and related accessories. It is a dynamic and complex industry influenced by various factors including legal regulations, technological advancements, consumer trends, and socio-political dynamics.

At its core, the firearms industry is driven by the production and distribution of firearms and ammunition. Manufacturers range from large-scale companies producing a wide range of firearms for military, law enforcement, and civilian use, to smaller boutique manufacturers specializing in custom firearms. These manufacturers utilize advanced technologies and precision engineering to design and produce firearms that meet the demands of different market segments.

Distribution channels play a crucial role in the firearms industry, connecting manufacturers with retailers and ultimately consumers. Firearms distributors serve as intermediaries, facilitating the movement of firearms and accessories from manufacturers to retail outlets. They often maintain extensive inventories and provide logistical support to ensure timely delivery of products to retailers.

Retailers, including gun stores, sporting goods stores, and online retailers, form the front line of the firearms industry, directly engaging with consumers. Gun stores, in particular, serve as hubs where consumers can purchase firearms, ammunition, and accessories, as well as seek advice and guidance from knowledgeable staff. These retail outlets cater to a diverse customer base ranging from shooting enthusiasts and hunters to law enforcement agencies and individuals seeking personal protection.

The firearms industry is also shaped by legal regulations at the federal, state, and local levels. Federal laws such as the Gun Control Act of 1968 and the National Firearms Act regulate the manufacture, sale, and possession of firearms and ammunition. State and local laws further govern aspects of firearm ownership and sales, including background checks, waiting periods, and restrictions on certain types of firearms.

In addition to legal regulations, the firearms industry is influenced by socio-political dynamics and cultural attitudes towards firearms. Debates over gun control, Second Amendment rights, and public safety shape public perception and influence consumer behavior. Changes in legislation and public opinion can have significant impacts on the firearms industry, driving shifts in demand, production, and marketing strategies.

Understanding the firearms industry requires a nuanced understanding of its various components, including manufacturing, distribution, retail, regulation, and socio-political factors. By grasping the complexities of the firearms industry, stakeholders can navigate its challenges and opportunities more effectively, contributing to the responsible and sustainable growth of the industry.

Historical Context and Evolution of Gun

The history of firearms is a fascinating journey that spans centuries and reflects the evolution of technology, warfare, and human civilization. The origins of firearms can be traced back to ancient China, where gunpowder was invented around the 9th century AD. Initially used for fireworks and ceremonial purposes, gunpowder eventually found its way into military applications, leading to the development of early firearms.

The earliest known firearms were simple devices known as "fire lances," which were essentially tubes filled with gunpowder and shrapnel. These early firearms were not very accurate or powerful but represented a significant technological advancement in warfare.

By the 14th century, firearms had evolved into more sophisticated weapons such as hand cannons and matchlock muskets. These early firearms were slow to reload and prone to misfires, but they were nonetheless effective in battle and gradually replaced traditional weapons like bows and crossbows.

The invention of the wheel-lock and flintlock mechanisms in the 16th and 17th centuries marked significant advancements in firearms technology. These mechanisms allowed for faster and more reliable ignition of gunpowder, making firearms more practical and reliable for military use.

During the 18th and 19th centuries, the Industrial Revolution fueled further advancements in firearms manufacturing and design. Innovations such as rifling, which improved accuracy, and interchangeable parts, which simplified maintenance and repair, transformed firearms into highly effective and versatile weapons.

The 19th century also saw the widespread adoption of breech-loading firearms, which allowed for faster reloading and increased rate of fire. This period also witnessed the introduction of metallic cartridges, which contained both the bullet and the propellant in a single unit, further enhancing the efficiency and convenience of firearms.

The late 19th and early 20th centuries brought about significant innovations in firearms design, including the development of semi-automatic and fully automatic firearms. These advancements revolutionized military tactics and warfare, leading to the widespread adoption of automatic weapons in armies around the world.

The 20th century also saw the rise of the firearms industry as a global business, with manufacturers producing a wide range of firearms for military, law enforcement, and civilian use. Technological advancements continued to drive innovation, with firearms becoming lighter, more accurate, and more reliable than ever before.

In recent decades, advancements in materials science, computer-aided design, and manufacturing technology have further transformed the firearms industry. Modern firearms are highly sophisticated weapons that incorporate advanced features such as optics, laser sights, and electronic firing mechanisms.

The historical context and evolution of firearms reflect the ingenuity and creativity of human beings in harnessing technology for both destructive and constructive purposes. From humble beginnings as simple tubes filled with gunpowder to the highly advanced weapons of today, firearms have played a pivotal role in shaping the course of history and continue to have a profound impact on society.

Purpose and Scope of This Book

The purpose of this book is to provide comprehensive guidance and practical insights for individuals interested in opening and operating a gun store. Whether you are a seasoned entrepreneur looking to enter the firearms industry or a passionate firearms enthusiast exploring the possibility of starting your own business, this book aims to equip you with the knowledge, resources, and strategies needed to succeed in the competitive landscape of the gun retailing sector.

Through a detailed examination of key topics such as regulatory compliance, market research, business planning, location selection, supplier relationships, store operations, marketing, customer service, financial management, and future growth strategies, this book offers a comprehensive roadmap for aspiring gun store owners.

The scope of this book encompasses a wide range of considerations and best practices relevant to establishing and managing a successful gun store business. It delves into the intricacies of navigating federal, state, and local regulations governing firearm sales and ensuring compliance with legal requirements. It also explores strategies for conducting market research, analyzing competition, and developing a robust business plan tailored to the unique needs of the firearms industry.

Additionally, this book addresses practical aspects of setting up a gun store, including selecting an optimal location, designing an effective store layout, establishing supplier relationships, and implementing sound operational and security measures. It offers insights into marketing and promotional strategies to attract customers, build brand awareness, and foster community engagement.

This book provides guidance on managing finances effectively, budgeting, forecasting, and ensuring regulatory compliance to promote the long-term sustainability and success of the gun store business. It also explores opportunities for future growth and expansion, including scaling operations, diversifying product offerings, and planning for continued success in an evolving industry landscape.

Understanding the Different Types of Guns, Ammunition, and Accessories:

Guns, ammunition, and accessories form the core components of the firearms industry, catering to diverse needs ranging from personal protection to recreational shooting and professional applications. Understanding the various types of guns, ammunition, and accessories is essential for both consumers and industry professionals.

Let's explore each category in detail:

1. Guns:

- **Handguns:** Handguns are firearms designed to be held and operated with one hand. They include pistols and revolvers, with variations such as semi-automatic, single-action, and double-action models.

- **Rifles:** Rifles are long-barreled firearms designed to be fired from the shoulder. They are characterized by their rifled barrels, which impart spin to the bullet for increased accuracy. Rifle types include bolt-action, semi-automatic, and lever-action rifles.

- **Shotguns:** Shotguns are firearms designed to fire a shell containing multiple pellets (shot) or a single projectile (slug). They are commonly used for hunting, sport shooting, and home defense. Shotgun variants include pump-action, semi-automatic, and break-action models.

2. Ammunition:

- **Handgun Ammunition:** Handgun ammunition is available in various calibers and configurations, including rim-fire and centerfire cartridges. Common handgun calibers include .22LR, 9mm, .45 ACP, and .357 Magnum.

- **Rifle Ammunition:** Rifle ammunition is designed for use in rifles and is available in a wide range of calibers and configurations, including rim-fire and centerfire cartridges. Common rifle calibers include .223 Remington, .308 Winchester, .30-06 Springfield, and 7.62x39mm.

- **Shotgun Ammunition:** Shotgun ammunition, also known as shotgun shells, is available in different gauges (e.g., 12 gauge, 20 gauge) and lengths (e.g., 2¾", 3", 3½"). Shotgun shells are loaded with various types of shot (e.g., birdshot, buckshot) or slugs for different applications.

3. Accessories:

- **Optics:** Optics, such as scopes, red dot sights, and holographic sights, enhance accuracy and target acquisition for rifles and handguns.

- **Holsters:** Holsters provide a safe and convenient method for carrying handguns, with options including inside-the-waistband (IWB), outside-the-waistband (OWB), and shoulder holsters.

- **Magazines:** Magazines are devices used to feed ammunition into firearms. They come in various capacities and configurations, including detachable box magazines and drum magazines.

- **Gun Cases:** Gun cases provide protection and storage for firearms during transportation and storage. They come in soft and hard-shell variants, with options for rifles, shotguns, and handguns.

Understanding the different types of guns, ammunition, and accessories enables consumers to make informed purchasing decisions based on their specific needs and preferences. It also provides industry professionals with essential knowledge for effectively serving their customers and meeting market demand.

The Importance of Responsible Gun Ownership

Responsible gun ownership is crucial for maintaining the safety and well-being of individuals, families, and communities. It encompasses a range of principles and practices aimed at ensuring that firearms are used and stored safely, legally, and ethically.

One of the primary reasons for promoting responsible gun ownership is to prevent accidents and injuries. Mishandling firearms or failing to follow proper safety protocols can lead to unintentional shootings, which often result in serious injury or death. By educating gun owners about safe handling practices, proper storage methods, and the importance of firearm safety devices such as gun locks and safes, responsible gun ownership helps minimize the risk of accidents and tragedies.

Responsible gun ownership contributes to public safety by reducing the likelihood of firearms falling into the wrong hands. Keeping firearms securely stored and out of reach of unauthorized individuals, especially children and individuals with mental health issues or criminal intentions, helps prevent unauthorized access and misuse of firearms. Responsible gun owners also play a crucial role in preventing theft by taking steps to secure their firearms and report lost or stolen weapons promptly.

Responsible gun ownership also involves complying with all applicable laws and regulations governing firearms. This includes obtaining the necessary licenses and permits, undergoing background checks when purchasing firearms, and adhering to restrictions on firearm possession and use in certain locations or circumstances. By following legal requirements and exercising good judgment, responsible gun owners contribute to a lawful and orderly society while minimizing the risk of criminal misuse of firearms.

Moreover, responsible gun ownership encompasses a commitment to ongoing education and training. Regular practice at shooting ranges, participation in firearms safety courses, and staying informed about changes in laws and regulations help gun owners develop and maintain the skills and knowledge necessary to handle firearms safely and responsibly. By continuously honing their skills and staying informed, responsible gun owners enhance their ability to handle firearms safely and effectively in various situations.

Another aspect of responsible gun ownership is promoting a culture of respect and accountability among gun owners. This involves fostering a sense of responsibility for the consequences of firearm use and advocating for safe and ethical behavior within the firearms community. By setting a positive example and encouraging others to prioritize safety and responsibility, responsible gun owners help create a culture where firearms are viewed as tools to be respected and used responsibly rather than objects of fear or violence.

Role of Gun Stores in Promoting Safety and Education

Gun stores play a crucial role in promoting safety and education within the firearms community and broader society. As hubs for firearm enthusiasts and individuals interested in purchasing firearms, ammunition, and accessories, gun stores have a unique opportunity to influence and shape responsible attitudes and behaviors related to firearms.

Here are several ways in which gun stores fulfill this role:

1. Education and Training: Gun stores often offer educational resources and training opportunities to customers, including firearm safety courses, introductory shooting classes, and advanced training seminars. These educational programs teach customers proper handling, storage, and use of firearms, as well as legal and ethical considerations related to firearm ownership. By providing access to quality education and training, gun stores empower customers to become knowledgeable and responsible gun owners.

2. Safety Equipment and Accessories: Gun stores typically offer a wide range of safety equipment and accessories designed to promote safe firearm handling and storage. This includes gun safes, lockboxes, trigger locks, and gun cases designed to secure firearms and prevent unauthorized access. By promoting and selling these safety products, gun stores encourage customers to take proactive steps to enhance firearm safety in their homes and communities.

3. Responsible Sales Practices: Ethical gun stores adhere to responsible sales practices, including conducting background checks and age verification for firearm purchases, as required by law. They also provide guidance and support to customers in selecting firearms that match their needs and experience levels, ensuring that customers are equipped with firearms that they can handle safely and responsibly. Additionally, responsible gun stores may implement policies to prevent straw purchases and unauthorized transactions, further promoting responsible firearm ownership.

4. Community Engagement: Many gun stores actively engage with their local communities through outreach programs, events, and partnerships with law enforcement agencies and community organizations. These initiatives may include hosting firearm safety seminars, participating in community events, and supporting youth shooting sports programs. By fostering positive relationships and promoting dialogue with the broader community, gun stores contribute to a culture of responsible firearm ownership and safety.

5. Advocacy and Awareness: Some gun stores take an active role in advocating for responsible firearm ownership and promoting awareness of safety issues within the firearms community. This may involve participating in public education campaigns, supporting initiatives to prevent firearm accidents and injuries, and advocating for legislative measures aimed at promoting safety and responsible gun ownership. By leveraging their influence and resources, gun stores can help raise awareness and promote positive change in attitudes and behaviors related to firearms.

How to Handle and Store Gun in a Responsible Way

Handling and storing guns in a responsible way is essential to ensure safety for yourself, your loved ones, and your community.

Here are some key principles to follow:

1. Education and Training:

 - Educate yourself about the safe handling and operation of firearms. Take a certified firearms safety course to learn about basic firearm safety rules, proper shooting techniques, and safe storage practices.

 - Practice regular firearm safety drills and review safety protocols with family members or household members who may have access to firearms.

2. Always Treat Firearms as if They Are Loaded:

 - Treat every firearm with the respect it deserves, and always assume that a firearm is loaded, even if you believe it to be unloaded.

 - Keep your finger off the trigger and outside the trigger guard until you are ready to shoot.

3. Keep Firearms Securely Stored:

- Store firearms in a secure location, such as a locked gun safe, gun cabinet, or lockbox, to prevent unauthorized access.

- Ensure that firearms are stored unloaded and with the ammunition stored separately in a locked container.

- Consider using additional safety devices such as trigger locks or cable locks to further secure firearms.

4. Store Ammunition Separately:

- Store ammunition in a separate, locked container from firearms to prevent unauthorized access.

- Keep ammunition stored in a cool, dry place away from heat sources and moisture to maintain its integrity.

5. Handle Firearms Safely:

- Always point the muzzle of the firearm in a safe direction, away from yourself and others, regardless of whether the firearm is loaded or unloaded.

- Keep the firearm's action open and the safety engaged when not in use.

- Never rely solely on the firearm's safety mechanism. Treat it as an additional safety measure, not a fail-safe mechanism.

6. Supervise and Educate Children:

- Educate children about the dangers of firearms and the importance of firearm safety.

- Supervise children closely when they are in the vicinity of firearms, and teach them to never handle firearms without adult supervision.

7. Be Mindful of Your Surroundings:

- Be aware of your surroundings and potential hazards when handling firearms, including other individuals, obstacles, and potential ricochets.

- Never shoot at hard surfaces or water, as bullets can ricochet unpredictably.

8. Follow Legal Requirements:

- Familiarize yourself with local, state, and federal laws and regulations governing the possession, storage, and transportation of firearms.

- Ensure compliance with all applicable laws, including obtaining the necessary permits and licenses for firearm ownership.

Understanding Regulations and Legal Requirements

Understanding regulations and legal requirements related to firearms is crucial for anyone involved in the firearms industry, including gun store owners, manufacturers, distributors, and individual gun owners. These regulations are established at the federal, state, and local levels and govern various aspects of firearms possession, sales, transportation, and use.

Federal regulations are established by agencies such as the Bureau of Alcohol, Tobacco, Firearms and Explosives (ATF) and the National Firearms Act (NFA). These regulations include requirements for obtaining a Federal Firearms License (FFL) to engage in the business of selling firearms, conducting background checks on firearm purchasers through the National Instant Criminal Background Check System (NICS), and adhering to specific record-keeping and reporting requirements for firearms transactions.

The Gun Control Act of 1968 (GCA) is one of the primary federal laws governing the firearms industry. It establishes criteria for firearm sales, prohibits certain individuals from possessing firearms, and regulates the importation and exportation of firearms and ammunition. The GCA also mandates the marking of firearms with a serial number and requires licensed firearms dealers to maintain records of firearms transactions.

The National Firearms Act (NFA) imposes additional regulations on certain types of firearms, including machine guns, short-barreled rifles, short-barreled shotguns, suppressors, and destructive devices such as grenades and bombs. Individuals and businesses seeking to possess or transfer NFA-regulated firearms must pay a tax and comply with specific registration and licensing requirements.

In addition to federal regulations, individual states and local jurisdictions may have their own laws and regulations governing firearms. These regulations can vary widely from state to state and may include requirements for firearm registration, licensing, and permits, as well as restrictions on the types of firearms that can be possessed or sold. Some states also impose waiting periods for firearm purchases and require background checks for private firearm transfers.

Understanding and complying with these regulations is essential for gun store owners to operate legally and avoid potential fines, penalties, or loss of their FFL. It is also important for individual gun owners to be aware of and adhere to applicable laws and regulations to ensure they remain in compliance and avoid legal consequences.

Understanding regulations and legal requirements related to firearms is essential for ensuring lawful and responsible behavior within the firearms industry and promoting public safety. By adhering to these regulations and taking appropriate measures to comply with legal requirements, individuals and businesses can help prevent firearms from falling into the wrong hands and contribute to a safer environment for all.

Federal Laws and Regulations

Federal laws and regulations pertaining to firearms in the United States are established and enforced primarily by agencies such as the Bureau of Alcohol, Tobacco, Firearms and Explosives (ATF), as well as through legislation passed by Congress. These federal laws and regulations are designed to regulate various aspects of firearms possession, sales, distribution, manufacturing, and use.

The Gun Control Act of 1968 (GCA) is one of the foundational pieces of federal legislation governing firearms. Enacted in response to increasing concerns about firearm-related crime and public safety, the GCA establishes a framework for regulating the firearms industry and sets forth criteria for the lawful sale and possession of firearms. Key provisions of the GCA include requirements for firearms dealers to obtain a Federal Firearms License (FFL), prohibitions on certain categories of individuals from possessing firearms (such as convicted felons, individuals adjudicated as mentally incompetent, and domestic violence offenders), and regulations governing the importation and exportation of firearms and ammunition.

The National Firearms Act (NFA) of 1934 is another important federal law that imposes additional regulations on certain types of firearms, including machine guns, short-barreled rifles (SBRs), short-barreled shotguns (SBSs), suppressors (silencers), and destructive devices such as grenades and bombs. Under the NFA, individuals and entities seeking to possess or transfer NFA-regulated firearms are required to pay a tax and comply with specific registration and licensing requirements, including the submission of fingerprints and photographs to the ATF, as well as the approval of the Chief Law Enforcement Officer (CLEO) in their jurisdiction.

Federal law also mandates the implementation of the National Instant Criminal Background Check System (NICS), which is administered by the FBI. The NICS is used to conduct background checks on individuals seeking to purchase firearms from federally licensed firearms dealers. The system is designed to identify individuals who are prohibited by law from possessing firearms, such as convicted felons, fugitives from justice, individuals subject to domestic violence restraining orders, and individuals with certain mental health adjudications.

Additionally, federal regulations issued by the ATF further clarify and enforce various provisions of federal firearms laws. These regulations cover a wide range of topics, including the marking of firearms with serial numbers, record-keeping and reporting requirements for firearms dealers, regulations governing the transportation and storage of firearms, and rules governing the manufacturing and distribution of firearms and ammunition.

Federal laws and regulations play a central role in regulating firearms in the United States, ensuring that firearms are lawfully and responsibly acquired, possessed, and used while also addressing public safety concerns and preventing firearms from falling into the wrong hands.

Overview of Federal Firearms License (FFL)

A Federal Firearms License (FFL) is a license issued by the Bureau of Alcohol, Tobacco, Firearms and Explosives (ATF) to individuals or entities engaged in the business of manufacturing, importing, or dealing in firearms and ammunition. The FFL system was established under the Gun Control Act of 1968 (GCA) to regulate and oversee the firearms industry in the United States.

There are several types of Federal Firearms Licenses, each corresponding to different activities within the firearms industry:

1. Type 01 FFL (Dealer in Firearms): This license authorizes individuals or entities to engage in the business of selling firearms and ammunition. Dealers with a Type 01 FFL can sell firearms to individuals, other FFL holders, and law enforcement agencies.

2. Type 02 FFL (Pawnbroker in Firearms): This license is issued to pawnbrokers who engage in the business of accepting firearms as collateral for loans or for resale.

3. Type 03 FFL (Collector of Curios and Relics): This license is issued to individuals who collect firearms classified as curios or relics, as defined by the ATF. Type 03 FFL holders can acquire certain firearms that are not available to the general public for collection and display purposes.

4. Type 06 FFL (Manufacturer of Ammunition for Firearms): This license authorizes individuals or entities to engage in the business of manufacturing ammunition for firearms.

5. Type 07 FFL (Manufacturer of Firearms): This license is issued to individuals or entities engaged in the business of manufacturing firearms, including assembling firearms from components, modifying firearms, or producing firearm frames or receivers.

6. Type 08 FFL (Importer of Firearms): This license is issued to individuals or entities engaged in the business of importing firearms and ammunition into the United States.

7. Type 09 FFL (Dealer in Destructive Devices): This license authorizes individuals or entities to engage in the business of selling destructive devices, such as explosives and certain types of firearms with bore diameters greater than one-half inch.

Obtaining an FFL requires applicants to meet certain eligibility criteria, including being at least 21 years of age (for Type 01, 02, 07, 08, and 09 licenses), not being prohibited from shipping, transporting, receiving, or possessing firearms or ammunition under federal law, and complying with all applicable state and local laws.

Applicants for an FFL must also submit an application to the ATF, undergo a background check, provide fingerprints, and pay the required application fee. Once approved, FFL holders must comply with all federal laws and regulations governing the firearms industry, including record-keeping and reporting requirements, conducting background checks on firearm purchasers, and adhering to restrictions on certain types of firearms and ammunition.

The Federal Firearms License (FFL) system plays a central role in regulating the firearms industry in the United States, ensuring that individuals and entities engaged in the business of manufacturing, importing, or dealing in firearms and ammunition do so in compliance with federal laws and regulations.

Compliance with ATF Regulations

Compliance with ATF regulations is essential for individuals and entities engaged in the firearms industry to ensure lawful and responsible conduct in accordance with federal laws. The Bureau of Alcohol, Tobacco, Firearms and Explosives (ATF) is the federal agency responsible for enforcing regulations related to firearms, explosives, arson, and alcohol and tobacco products.

ATF regulations cover a wide range of areas within the firearms industry, including manufacturing, importing, distributing, and selling firearms and ammunition. Compliance with ATF regulations is mandatory for all individuals and entities holding a Federal Firearms License (FFL) and engaging in activities regulated by the ATF.

Some key areas of compliance with ATF regulations include:

1. Record-keeping and reporting: FFL holders are required to maintain accurate and up-to-date records of all firearms transactions, including the acquisition and disposition of firearms. This includes recording the make, model, and serial number of each firearm, as well as information about the buyer or transferee. FFL holders must also report certain firearms transactions to the ATF, such as multiple handgun sales to the same individual within a five-day period.

2. Background Checks: FFL holders are required to conduct background checks on individuals seeking to purchase firearms from their licensed premises, in accordance with the National Instant Criminal Background Check System (NICS). This includes verifying the identity of the purchaser, conducting a background check to determine whether the purchaser is prohibited from possessing firearms under federal or state law, and documenting the results of the background check.

3. Security Measures: FFL holders are required to implement security measures to prevent theft or loss of firearms from their licensed premises. This includes securing firearms in locked cabinets or safes when not in use, installing security alarms and surveillance cameras, and implementing procedures to monitor and control access to firearms.

4. Prohibited Persons: FFL holders are prohibited from selling or transferring firearms to individuals who are prohibited from possessing firearms under federal or state law. This includes individuals who have been convicted of certain crimes, adjudicated as mentally incompetent, subject to certain domestic violence restraining orders, or unlawfully present in the United States.

5. Compliance Inspections: The ATF conducts routine compliance inspections of FFL holders to ensure compliance with federal firearms laws and regulations. During these inspections, ATF agents review records, inventory firearms, and assess the licensee's compliance with security and record-keeping requirements. FFL holders are required to cooperate fully with ATF inspections and provide access to all relevant records and premises.

Compliance with ATF regulations is essential for FFL holders to maintain their license and operate legally within the firearms industry. By adhering to ATF regulations, FFL holders contribute to public safety and the responsible conduct of firearms-related activities, while also ensuring their own legal and regulatory compliance.

Navigating the National Firearms Act (NFA)

The National Firearms Act (NFA) is a federal law enacted in 1934 that regulates the possession, transfer, and taxation of certain types of firearms and devices considered to be particularly dangerous or unusual. The NFA imposes stringent regulations on firearms such as machine guns, short-barreled rifles (SBRs), short-barreled shotguns (SBSs), suppressors (silencers), and destructive devices such as grenades and bombs.

Navigating the NFA involves understanding its provisions, complying with its requirements, and adhering to the legal framework established by the law. Key aspects of navigating the NFA include:

- **Understanding Regulated Items:** The NFA regulates specific categories of firearms and devices, including machine guns, SBRs, SBSs, suppressors, and destructive devices. These items are subject to special regulations and restrictions under the law.

- **Tax Stamp Requirements:** Under the NFA, individuals or entities seeking to possess or transfer NFA-regulated firearms or devices must pay a tax and obtain approval from the Bureau of Alcohol, Tobacco, Firearms and Explosives (ATF). This typically involves submitting an application, fingerprints, and photographs, as well as paying a tax stamp fee.

- **Registration and Licensing:** NFA-regulated firearms and devices must be registered with the ATF, and individuals or entities in possession of these items must hold the appropriate licenses or permits, such as a Federal Firearms License (FFL) or a Special Occupational Tax (SOT) stamp for certain types of dealers and manufacturers.

- **Compliance with Transfer Restrictions:** The NFA imposes restrictions on the transfer and possession of NFA-regulated firearms and devices. Transfers of these items must be conducted through the ATF's NFA registry, and individuals or entities involved in the transfer must comply with all applicable regulations and requirements.

- **Safe Storage and Transportation:** NFA-regulated firearms and devices must be stored and transported in compliance with federal and state laws. This may include storing these items securely in a locked container or safe and adhering to specific transportation requirements when transporting them between locations.

- **Record-keeping and Reporting:** Individuals or entities in possession of NFA-regulated firearms and devices must maintain accurate records of these items and report certain transactions to the ATF. This includes documenting the acquisition and disposition of NFA items and complying with record-keeping requirements specified by the ATF.

Navigating the National Firearms Act (NFA) involves understanding its provisions, complying with its requirements, and ensuring legal and responsible conduct related to the possession, transfer, and taxation of NFA-regulated firearms and devices. By adhering to the legal framework established by the NFA, individuals and entities can navigate the complexities of the law and operate within the bounds of federal firearms regulations.

State Laws and Regulations

State laws and regulations pertaining to firearms vary widely across the United States, and individuals involved in the firearms industry must navigate these diverse legal frameworks to ensure compliance with state-specific requirements. State laws and regulations often address a range of issues related to firearms, including licensing and permitting, background checks, firearm sales and transfers, possession and carrying of firearms, and restrictions on certain types of firearms and accessories.

Some states have enacted stricter regulations on firearms ownership and possession than others, imposing requirements such as waiting periods for firearm purchases, mandatory background checks for all firearm transfers (including private sales), and restrictions on the types of firearms that can be legally owned or carried in public. For example, certain states may prohibit the sale or possession of assault weapons or large-capacity magazines, while others may impose additional licensing or registration requirements for certain types of firearms or accessories.

In addition to regulating firearm ownership and possession, state laws may also address issues related to firearm sales and transfers, including requirements for conducting background checks on firearm purchasers, maintaining records of firearm transactions, and regulating the sale of firearms at gun shows or through online platforms.

State laws also govern the carrying of firearms in public places, including restrictions on where firearms can be carried (e.g., schools, government buildings, places of worship), requirements for obtaining a concealed carry permit or license, and regulations governing the open carrying of firearms in public.

Firearm owners and industry professionals must also be aware of any restrictions or regulations specific to certain types of firearms or accessories, such as suppressors (silencers), high-capacity magazines, and firearms classified as "assault weapons" or "restricted firearms" under state law.

Navigating state laws and regulations requires individuals and entities in the firearms industry to stay informed about changes in state law, understand the specific requirements applicable to their jurisdiction, and ensure compliance with all relevant legal requirements. This may involve consulting with legal counsel, obtaining the necessary permits or licenses, conducting background checks and record-keeping as required by law, and adhering to restrictions on firearm sales, transfers, and possession imposed by state law.

Researching State-Specific Requirements

Researching state-specific requirements related to firearms involves gathering information on relevant laws, regulations, and administrative procedures specific to each state. This process typically includes several key steps:

1. Identifying Relevant Authorities: Begin by identifying the state-level authorities responsible for regulating firearms within the state. This may include agencies such as the state's department of justice, department of public safety, or state police.

2. Accessing Official Sources: Visit the official website of the state government or the relevant state agency responsible for firearms regulation. These websites often provide comprehensive information on state laws, regulations, and administrative procedures related to firearms.

3. Reviewing Statutes and Regulations: Research the state's statutes (laws) and administrative regulations governing firearms. State statutes are typically published in the state's legal code, while administrative regulations are often found in the state's administrative code. Online databases such as LexisNexis, Westlaw, or the state legislature's website may provide access to these legal resources.

4. Identifying Key Legal Provisions: Identify key legal provisions related to firearms ownership, possession, carrying, sales, transfers, licensing, and registration within the state. Pay attention to any specific requirements or restrictions imposed by state law, such as waiting periods for firearm purchases, background check requirements, and restrictions on certain types of firearms or accessories.

5. Consulting Legal Resources: Consider consulting legal resources such as legal guides, handbooks, or online legal databases that provide analysis and interpretation of state firearms laws. Legal resources specific to firearms law may offer insights into the practical implications of state laws and regulations and help clarify any legal ambiguities.

6. Seeking Clarification from Authorities: If you encounter uncertainties or have specific questions about state firearms laws and regulations, consider reaching out to state-level authorities responsible for firearms regulation, such as the state's department of justice or state police. These authorities may provide guidance or clarification on state-specific requirements and procedures.

7. Staying Updated: Keep abreast of any changes or updates to state firearms laws and regulations. State legislatures regularly introduce new legislation, amend existing laws, or promulgate new administrative regulations that may impact firearms regulation within the state. Monitoring legislative updates and staying informed about changes in state law is essential for maintaining compliance with state-specific requirements.

Licensing and Permits

Licensing and permits play a crucial role in regulating firearms ownership, possession, and carrying, as well as in ensuring public safety and preventing unauthorized access to firearms. Licensing and permit requirements vary widely across different jurisdictions and may include the following components:

1. Firearm Ownership Licenses: Some states require individuals to obtain a license or permit to own firearms. These licenses, often referred to as firearm owner identification cards (FOID) or firearm purchase permits, may be issued by state or local law enforcement agencies and require applicants to undergo a background check and meet certain eligibility criteria.

2. Concealed Carry Permits: Many states require individuals to obtain a concealed carry permit (also known as a concealed handgun license or concealed carry weapon permit) to carry a concealed firearm in public places. Concealed carry permits typically require applicants to complete a firearms training course, undergo a background check, and demonstrate a legitimate need or justification for carrying a concealed firearm.

3. Open Carry Permits: Some states allow individuals to openly carry firearms in public places without a permit, while others require individuals to obtain an open carry permit or license to openly carry firearms. Open carry permits may impose additional requirements such as background checks, training courses, or restrictions on where firearms can be openly carried.

4. Dealer Licenses: Federal law requires individuals or entities engaged in the business of selling firearms to obtain a Federal Firearms License (FFL) from the Bureau of Alcohol, Tobacco, Firearms and Explosives (ATF). In addition to federal licensing requirements, many states also impose licensing or registration requirements on firearms dealers, including background checks, record-keeping requirements, and compliance with state and local laws.

5. Ammunition Sales Permits: Some states require individuals or entities engaged in the business of selling ammunition to obtain a separate permit or license to sell ammunition. These permits may be issued by state or local authorities and may include requirements such as background checks, record-keeping requirements, and compliance with state laws regulating ammunition sales.

6. Firearm Training and Safety Certificates: Some states require individuals to complete a firearms training or safety course and obtain a certificate of completion before obtaining a concealed carry permit or purchasing a firearm. These training courses typically cover topics such as firearm safety, basic firearm handling, marksmanship, and legal aspects of firearm ownership and use.

Compliance with Local Ordinances

Compliance with local ordinances is essential for individuals and entities involved in the firearms industry to ensure adherence to regulations imposed by local governments, such as cities, counties, or municipalities. Local ordinances may supplement or further specify requirements established by state or federal law, addressing specific concerns or circumstances within a particular jurisdiction. Compliance with local ordinances typically involves several key considerations:

1. Researching Local Ordinances: Begin by researching local ordinances relevant to firearms ownership, possession, sales, and carrying within the jurisdiction where you reside or conduct business. Local ordinances may be accessible through the official website of the local government or by contacting the relevant municipal authorities.

2. Understanding Specific Requirements: Review local ordinances to understand specific requirements and restrictions imposed on firearms-related activities within the jurisdiction. This may include regulations governing the storage and transportation of firearms, restrictions on the discharge of firearms within city limits, zoning restrictions on firearms-related businesses, and limitations on where firearms can be carried in public places.

3. Obtaining Necessary Permits or Licenses: Determine whether any permits or licenses are required under local ordinances to engage in firearms-related activities, such as operating a firearms dealership or conducting firearms training courses. Obtain the necessary permits or licenses from the local government or relevant authorities as required by local ordinances.

4. Compliance with Zoning Regulations: Ensure compliance with any zoning regulations imposed by local ordinances on firearms-related businesses, shooting ranges, or other facilities. Zoning regulations may dictate where firearms-related businesses can be located within the jurisdiction and may impose certain restrictions or requirements on these establishments.

5. Keeping Abreast of Changes: Stay informed about any changes or updates to local ordinances related to firearms regulation. Local governments may introduce new ordinances, amend existing regulations, or adopt additional restrictions on firearms-related activities within the jurisdiction. Monitoring local government proceedings and staying informed about changes in local law is essential for maintaining compliance with local ordinances.

6. Consulting Legal Counsel: Consider consulting with legal counsel or knowledgeable professionals familiar with local firearms regulations to ensure understanding and compliance with local ordinances. Legal counsel can provide guidance on interpreting local ordinances, navigating legal requirements, and addressing any compliance issues or concerns that may arise.

Compliance with local ordinances is crucial for individuals and entities involved in the firearms industry to operate legally and responsibly within their respective jurisdictions. By understanding and adhering to local ordinances, individuals and entities can ensure compliance with legal requirements, promote public safety, and avoid potential penalties or legal consequences associated with non-compliance.

Market Research and Business Planning

Market research and business planning are essential components of establishing and operating a successful gun store or firearms-related business. These processes involve gathering and analyzing information about the firearms industry, identifying target markets and customer demographics, assessing competition, and developing a strategic plan to launch and grow the business. Here are some key considerations:

Market Research:

- Conduct thorough research on the firearms industry, including trends, market size, and growth projections. Analyze industry reports, trade publications, and market research studies to gain insights into consumer preferences, purchasing behavior, and market dynamics.

- Identify target markets and customer segments for the gun store, such as firearm enthusiasts, hunters, sports shooters, law enforcement personnel, and security professionals. Understand their needs, preferences, and purchasing habits to tailor products and services accordingly.

- Analyze the competitive landscape by researching existing gun stores and firearms-related businesses in the area. Assess their offerings, pricing strategies, marketing tactics, and customer service to identify strengths, weaknesses, and opportunities for differentiation.

- Evaluate regulatory requirements and compliance considerations specific to the firearms industry, including federal, state, and local laws governing firearm sales, background checks, licensing, and permits. Ensure compliance with all legal and regulatory requirements to operate the business lawfully.

Business Planning:

- Develop a comprehensive business plan outlining the vision, mission, goals, and objectives of the gun store or firearms-related business. Define the business model, target market, product offerings, pricing strategy, marketing plan, and sales projections.

- Determine the location of the gun store based on market research, demographic analysis, and accessibility to target customers. Consider factors such as foot traffic, visibility, parking, and proximity to shooting ranges or other complementary businesses.

- Create a budget and financial plan detailing startup costs, operating expenses, inventory investment, and revenue projections. Identify potential sources of funding, such as personal savings, loans, investors, or partnerships, to finance the startup and ongoing operations.

- Develop a marketing plan to promote the gun store and attract customers. Utilize a mix of marketing channels, including online advertising, social media marketing, search engine optimization (SEO), email marketing, direct mail, and local advertising, to reach target customers and build brand awareness.

- Establish relationships with firearms manufacturers, distributors, and suppliers to source inventory and negotiate favorable terms. Build a diverse product assortment catering to the needs and preferences of target customers, including firearms, ammunition, accessories, and related gear.

- Hire qualified staff with expertise in firearms sales, customer service, and compliance to provide a positive shopping experience for customers. Provide training and ongoing support to staff to ensure product knowledge, safety awareness, and compliance with legal and regulatory requirements.

- Implement systems and processes for inventory management, sales transactions, background checks, and record-keeping to streamline operations and ensure accuracy, efficiency, and compliance with regulatory requirements.

Conducting thorough market research and developing a comprehensive business plan, gun store owners and firearms-related businesses can position themselves for success in the competitive firearms industry. A well-defined strategy, coupled with effective execution and a commitment to compliance, can help drive growth, profitability, and customer satisfaction in the firearms business.

Identifying Target Market

Identifying the target market is a critical step in the process of establishing and operating a successful gun store or firearms-related business. The target market refers to the specific group of consumers or organizations that the business aims to serve with its products or services. Identifying the target market involves understanding their needs, preferences, behaviors, and characteristics to tailor offerings and marketing efforts accordingly.

To identify the target market for a gun store or firearms-related business, several key considerations should be taken into account:

1. Demographic Factors: Consider demographic factors such as age, gender, income level, occupation, education, and geographic location. Determine which demographic segments are most likely to have an interest in firearms and related products, such as firearm enthusiasts, hunters, sports shooters, law enforcement personnel, security professionals, and individuals interested in self-defense.

2. Psychographic Factors: Assess psychographic factors such as lifestyle, values, attitudes, interests, and personality traits. Identify psychographic segments that align with the values and interests associated with firearms ownership and participation in shooting sports or recreational shooting activities.

3. Behavioral Factors: Analyze behavioral factors such as purchasing behavior, buying frequency, brand loyalty, and product usage. Determine the behaviors and purchasing patterns of potential customers related to firearms and related products, including their willingness to invest in firearms, ammunition, accessories, and training.

4. Needs and Preferences: Understand the needs, preferences, and motivations of the target market regarding firearms ownership and use. Identify the specific types of firearms, ammunition, accessories, and related gear that are most relevant and desirable to the target market, based on their intended use, shooting preferences, and personal preferences.

5. Competitive Analysis: Conduct a competitive analysis to assess the offerings, strengths, weaknesses, and market positioning of existing gun stores and firearms-related businesses in the area. Identify gaps or opportunities in the market that can be leveraged to differentiate the business and attract the target market.

6. Customer Feedback: Gather feedback from existing customers or potential customers through surveys, focus groups, interviews, or online reviews. Solicit feedback on their experiences, preferences, and unmet needs related to firearms ownership, purchasing, and usage. Use this feedback to refine the target market profile and tailor offerings to better meet customer needs.

7. Trends and Market Dynamics: Stay informed about industry trends, market dynamics, and emerging developments in the firearms industry. Monitor changes in consumer behavior, regulatory requirements, technological advancements, and competitive landscape to adapt strategies and offerings accordingly and remain relevant to the target market.

Carefully analyze demographic, psychographic, and behavioral factors, as well as competitive dynamics and customer feedback, gun store owners and firearms-related businesses can effectively identify their target market and develop strategies to attract, serve, and retain customers within this segment. Tailoring offerings, marketing messages, and customer experiences to meet the needs and preferences of the target market can help drive business growth, profitability, and customer satisfaction in the competitive firearms industry.

Analyzing Competitors

Analyzing competitors is a crucial aspect of market research and business planning for gun stores or firearms-related businesses. By understanding the strengths, weaknesses, strategies, and market positioning of competitors, businesses can identify opportunities for differentiation, develop effective marketing strategies, and make informed decisions to gain a competitive edge in the market.

To analyze competitors effectively, businesses should consider the following key aspects:

1. Product and Service Offerings: Examine the product and service offerings of competitors, including the types of firearms, ammunition, accessories, and related gear they sell, as well as any additional services they offer such as gunsmithing, firearm customization, or training courses. Evaluate the quality, variety, and pricing of their offerings to understand how they compare to your own.

2. Pricing Strategy: Assess the pricing strategy employed by competitors, including their pricing levels for different products and services, discounts, promotions, and pricing structures. Compare their pricing to your own to identify opportunities for competitive pricing positioning or adjustments to remain competitive in the market.

3. Target Market and Customer Base: Identify the target market and customer base of competitors, including demographic, psychographic, and behavioral characteristics of their customers. Understand their customer preferences, needs, and purchasing behavior to identify potential areas of overlap or differentiation in target markets.

4. Brand Positioning and Messaging: Evaluate the brand positioning and messaging of competitors, including their brand identity, value proposition, marketing messages, and positioning in the market. Assess how competitors differentiate themselves from others and communicate their unique selling points to customers.

5. Marketing and Promotion Strategies: Analyze the marketing and promotion strategies used by competitors, including their advertising channels, promotional tactics, digital marketing efforts, social media presence, and community engagement. Evaluate the effectiveness of their marketing campaigns and strategies in reaching and engaging target customers.

6. Customer Experience and Satisfaction: Assess the customer experience and satisfaction provided by competitors, including factors such as customer service quality, responsiveness, reliability, and satisfaction levels among their customer base. Gather feedback from customers and online reviews to understand their experiences and perceptions of competitors.

7. Strengths and Weaknesses: Identify the strengths and weaknesses of competitors relative to your own business, including factors such as product selection, pricing, customer service, brand reputation, market presence, and competitive advantages. Evaluate areas where competitors excel and areas where they may be vulnerable to competition.

8. Market Share and Growth Potential: Estimate the market share and growth potential of competitors within the firearms industry, including their market presence, sales volume, market share relative to other competitors, and growth trajectory. Understand the competitive landscape and identify opportunities to gain market share or enter untapped market segments.

Creating a Business Plan

Creating a business plan is a crucial step in establishing and operating a successful gun store or firearms-related business. A well-developed business plan serves as a roadmap for the business, outlining its vision, mission, goals, objectives, strategies, and operational details. It provides a comprehensive framework for guiding decision-making, securing financing, attracting investors, and achieving long-term success.

Here are the key components of creating a business plan:

1. Executive Summary: The executive summary provides an overview of the business plan, summarizing key elements such as the business concept, market opportunity, target market, competitive advantage, financial projections, and funding requirements. It serves as a concise introduction to the business plan and highlights the business's value proposition and potential for success.

2. Business Description: The business description provides detailed information about the gun store or firearms-related business, including its legal structure, ownership, location, facilities, and history. It outlines the business's mission, vision, values, and goals, as well as its unique selling proposition and competitive advantage in the market.

3. Market Analysis: The market analysis section examines the firearms industry and market opportunity, including trends, growth projections, target market segments, customer demographics, and competitive landscape. It analyzes factors such as consumer demand, purchasing behavior, regulatory environment, and market dynamics to assess the viability of the business concept and identify opportunities for growth and differentiation.

4. Products and Services: The products and services section describes the range of firearms, ammunition, accessories, and related products or services offered by the business. It outlines the features, benefits, pricing, and positioning of the products and services, as well as any unique offerings or value-added services that differentiate the business from competitors.

5. Marketing and Sales Strategy: The marketing and sales strategy outlines how the business plans to attract and retain customers, generate sales, and achieve revenue targets. It includes strategies for branding, advertising, promotions, digital marketing, social media, public relations, and customer acquisition. It also outlines the sales process, distribution channels, pricing strategy, and customer relationship management.

6. Operations and Management: The operations and management section details the operational structure and management team of the business. It outlines the organizational structure, roles and responsibilities of key personnel, staffing requirements, and operational processes. It also addresses key operational considerations such as inventory management, supplier relationships, regulatory compliance, and customer service.

7. Financial Plan: The financial plan provides a comprehensive overview of the financial aspects of the business, including startup costs, funding requirements, revenue projections, expense forecasts, and profit margins. It includes a detailed breakdown of expenses such as rent, utilities, payroll, inventory, marketing, and administrative costs. It also includes cash flow projections, balance sheets, income statements, and financial ratios to assess the financial health and viability of the business.

8. Funding Requirements: The funding requirements section outlines the capital needed to start and operate the business, including startup costs, working capital, and ongoing expenses. It identifies potential sources of funding, such as personal savings, loans, investors, or partnerships, and outlines the terms and conditions of financing arrangements.

9. Risk Management: The risk management section identifies potential risks and challenges that may impact the success of the business and outlines strategies for mitigating and managing these risks. It addresses factors such as regulatory compliance, market volatility, competitive pressures, operational challenges, and financial risks, and outlines contingency plans and risk mitigation strategies to minimize exposure and protect the business.

Executive Summary

The executive summary is a concise overview of the entire business plan, providing a snapshot of the key elements and highlights to investors, stakeholders, and potential partners. It serves as the first section of the business plan and is typically written last, after all other sections have been completed. The executive summary should capture the essence of the business plan and compel readers to delve deeper into the details of the plan.

In the executive summary, the business concept and value proposition are articulated succinctly, emphasizing what sets the business apart in the market and why it is poised for success. It outlines the market opportunity and target market segments, highlighting the potential for growth and profitability. The executive summary also introduces the management team and their qualifications, demonstrating their ability to execute the business plan effectively.

Key financial highlights and projections are summarized in the executive summary, providing an overview of the business's revenue potential, profitability, and return on investment. Funding requirements and sources of financing are outlined, indicating the capital needed to start and operate the business and the potential for investors to participate in the venture.

The executive summary encapsulates the vision, mission, and goals of the business, conveying a sense of purpose and direction. It communicates the business's unique selling proposition and competitive advantage, distinguishing it from competitors and compelling customers to choose the business's products or services. The executive summary also highlights key milestones and objectives, illustrating the roadmap for achieving success and capturing market share.

Company Description

The company description section of a business plan provides an in-depth overview of the gun store or firearms-related business, outlining its purpose, history, structure, and core attributes. This section serves to introduce the business to investors, stakeholders, and potential partners, providing essential context and background information.

In the company description, the business's legal structure and ownership are outlined, including whether it is a sole proprietorship, partnership, corporation, or limited liability company (LLC). The ownership structure and key stakeholders are identified, along with their roles and responsibilities within the business.

The history of the business is detailed, highlighting its origins, founding members, and significant milestones or achievements. This may include information about the inspiration behind starting the business, the founders' backgrounds and expertise in the firearms industry, and any notable accomplishments or recognitions received by the business.

The mission, vision, and values of the business are articulated, conveying its overarching purpose, long-term objectives, and guiding principles. The mission statement communicates the core purpose of the business and its commitment to serving customers, while the vision statement outlines its aspirations and goals for the future. The company's values reflect its ethical principles, beliefs, and priorities, guiding decision-making and shaping its organizational culture.

The unique selling proposition (USP) and competitive advantage of the business are emphasized, highlighting what sets it apart from competitors and why customers should choose its products or services. This may include factors such as specialized expertise in firearms sales, a unique product offering, exceptional customer service, competitive pricing, or a strategic location.

The company description also provides an overview of the business's target market and customer segments, identifying the demographic, psychographic, and behavioral characteristics of its ideal customers. This includes information about the size and growth potential of the target market, key customer needs and preferences, and strategies for attracting and retaining customers.

The company description serves as a comprehensive introduction to the gun store or firearms-related business, providing essential context and background information to stakeholders. It conveys the business's purpose, history, structure, mission, vision, values, unique selling proposition, and target market, laying the foundation for the rest of the business plan.

Market Analysis

Market analysis is a critical component of the business planning process for gun stores or firearms-related businesses. It involves thorough research and assessment of the firearms industry, market trends, customer demographics, competitive landscape, regulatory environment, and other factors that may impact the success of the business. A comprehensive market analysis provides valuable insights into the market opportunity, customer needs and preferences, competitive dynamics, and growth potential, guiding strategic decision-making and business planning.

In the market analysis, the firearms industry is examined in detail, including its size, scope, and growth projections. This involves analyzing industry reports, market research studies, and trade publications to understand key trends, emerging developments, and market dynamics shaping the firearms industry. Factors such as changes in consumer preferences, advancements in firearm technology, regulatory developments, and economic trends are considered to assess the overall health and trajectory of the industry.

The market opportunity for the gun store or firearms-related business is evaluated, including the demand for firearms, ammunition, accessories, and related products or services. This involves identifying target market segments and customer demographics that are most likely to purchase firearms or engage in shooting sports or recreational shooting activities. Factors such as demographic trends, lifestyle preferences, cultural influences, and geographic considerations are analyzed to determine the size and growth potential of the target market.

Customer needs and preferences within the firearms industry are explored, including factors such as product preferences, purchasing behavior, brand loyalty, and decision-making criteria. This involves gathering insights from customer surveys, focus groups, interviews, and online reviews to understand customer motivations, pain points, and unmet needs related to firearms ownership, purchasing, and usage. By understanding customer needs and preferences, businesses can tailor their offerings and marketing efforts to better meet customer expectations and drive sales.

The competitive landscape of the firearms industry is assessed, including the strengths, weaknesses, strategies, and market positioning of competitors. This involves conducting a competitive analysis to identify existing gun stores and firearms-related businesses in the area, as well as their offerings, pricing strategies, marketing tactics, and customer service. By understanding the competitive landscape, businesses can identify opportunities for differentiation and develop strategies to position themselves effectively in the market.

Regulatory and legal considerations specific to the firearms industry are also addressed in the market analysis. This includes analyzing federal, state, and local laws governing firearm sales, background checks, licensing, permits, and other regulatory requirements. By understanding regulatory requirements and compliance considerations, businesses can ensure legal compliance and mitigate regulatory risks associated with operating in the firearms industry.

A comprehensive market analysis provides valuable insights into the firearms industry, market opportunity, customer needs and preferences, competitive landscape, and regulatory environment. By conducting thorough research and assessment, businesses can identify opportunities for growth and differentiation, develop targeted strategies to attract and retain customers, and navigate regulatory requirements to operate successfully in the competitive firearms market.

Organization and Management Structure

The organization and management structure section of a business plan provides an overview of the organizational framework and leadership team of the gun store or firearms-related business. This section outlines the key personnel, their roles and responsibilities, and the organizational hierarchy, demonstrating the business's ability to effectively manage operations and execute its strategic objectives.

The organizational structure of the business is described, including its legal structure (e.g., sole proprietorship, partnership, corporation, Limited Liability Company) and ownership details. This outlines how the business is legally organized and the ownership distribution among partners or shareholders, if applicable.

The management team is introduced, highlighting the qualifications, expertise, and experience of key personnel responsible for overseeing day-to-day operations and strategic decision-making. This includes the founder(s), owner(s), executives, managers, and other key employees involved in running the business.

The roles and responsibilities of key personnel are outlined, detailing their specific areas of expertise and contributions to the business. This includes responsibilities such as operations management, sales and marketing, finance and accounting, human resources, customer service, and regulatory compliance.

The organizational hierarchy is illustrated, showing the reporting relationships and chain of command within the business. This outlines the structure of decision-making and communication flow among different levels of management and staff, ensuring clarity and accountability in executing business operations.

Key personnel's relevant experience and qualifications are highlighted, including their professional backgrounds, educational credentials, industry certifications, and any specialized training or expertise related to the firearms industry. This demonstrates the leadership team's ability to effectively manage the business and navigate challenges in the industry.

Any advisory board members, consultants, or external advisors who provide strategic guidance and support to the business are also mentioned. This includes individuals with expertise in areas such as legal affairs, finance, marketing, operations, or regulatory compliance, who contribute valuable insights and advice to the management team.

The organization and management structure section of the business plan provides a comprehensive overview of the business's leadership team, organizational framework, and decision-making processes. It demonstrates the business's capacity to effectively manage operations, execute its strategic objectives, and navigate challenges in the competitive firearms industry.

Marketing and Sales Strategies

Marketing and sales strategies are essential components of the business plan for gun stores or firearms-related businesses. These strategies outline how the business plans to attract customers, generate sales, and achieve revenue targets by effectively promoting its products and services in the market.

The marketing strategy: Involves identifying target market segments and developing tailored marketing initiatives to reach and engage these customers. This includes understanding the demographic, psychographic, and behavioral characteristics of the target market and designing marketing messages and campaigns that resonate with their needs, preferences, and interests.

The marketing mix is defined, outlining the various elements of the marketing strategy, including product, price, place, and promotion. This involves determining the product offerings, pricing strategy, distribution channels, and promotional tactics that will be used to attract customers and drive sales.

Product strategy: Focuses on the range of firearms, ammunition, accessories, and related products or services offered by the business. This includes identifying the product categories, brands, models, and features that appeal to target customers and align with their needs and preferences.

Pricing strategy: Involves determining the pricing levels for different products and services offered by the business. This includes considering factors such as production costs, competitor pricing, market demand, and customer perception to set competitive and profitable pricing levels that maximize revenue and profitability.

Place strategy: Involves selecting the distribution channels through which the business will sell its products and services to customers. This includes determining whether sales will be conducted through a physical storefront, online platform, distribution partners, or other channels, and ensuring that products are available and accessible to customers in the target market.

Promotion strategy: Encompasses the various marketing tactics and channels used to promote the business and its offerings to target customers. This includes advertising, public relations, digital marketing, social media, content marketing, email marketing, direct mail, events, and other promotional activities designed to raise awareness, generate interest, and drive sales.

Sales strategy: Focuses on the tactics and processes used to convert leads and prospects into paying customers. This includes developing a sales process, training sales staff, setting sales targets, implementing customer relationship management (CRM) systems, and tracking sales performance to optimize sales effectiveness and efficiency.

The marketing and sales strategies outlined in the business plan are designed to attract customers, generate sales, and drive business growth by effectively promoting the business's products and services in the competitive firearms market. These strategies are informed by a deep understanding of the target market, competitive landscape, and industry dynamics, and are executed with a focus on delivering value and building strong customer relationships.

Financial Projections

Financial projections are a critical component of the business plan for gun stores or firearms-related businesses, providing a detailed forecast of the business's financial performance over a specified period. These projections help investors, stakeholders, and lenders assess the business's revenue potential, profitability, and financial viability, and guide strategic decision-making and resource allocation.

Financial projections typically include three key financial statements: the income statement, balance sheet, and cash flow statement. These statements provide a comprehensive overview of the business's financial health, including its revenue, expenses, assets, liabilities, and cash flow.

The income statement, also known as the profit and loss (P&L) statement, provides a summary of the business's revenues and expenses over a specific period, typically monthly or annually. It outlines the business's total sales revenue, cost of goods sold (COGS), gross profit margin, operating expenses, net profit or loss, and earnings before interest, taxes, depreciation, and amortization (EBITDA). The income statement reflects the business's ability to generate profits from its operations and is used to assess its profitability and financial performance.

The balance sheet provides a snapshot of the business's financial position at a specific point in time, typically at the end of a reporting period. It outlines the business's assets, liabilities, and shareholders' equity, reflecting its financial resources and obligations. The balance sheet includes categories such as current assets (e.g., cash, inventory, accounts receivable), fixed assets (e.g., property, equipment, vehicles), current liabilities (e.g., accounts payable, accrued expenses), long-term liabilities (e.g., loans, mortgages), and shareholders' equity (e.g., retained earnings, capital contributions). The balance sheet helps assess the business's liquidity, solvency, and financial stability.

The cash flow statement provides a summary of the business's cash inflows and outflows over a specific period, typically monthly or annually. It outlines the sources and uses of cash, including cash flows from operating activities (e.g., sales revenue, operating expenses), investing activities (e.g., purchase of equipment, investments), and financing activities (e.g., loans, capital contributions). The cash flow statement reflects the business's ability to generate and manage cash, and is used to assess its liquidity and cash flow management.

Financial projections are typically based on assumptions and estimates about future performance, including sales forecasts, expense projections, pricing assumptions, market trends, and economic conditions. These assumptions are supported by market research, historical data, industry benchmarks, and expert judgment, and are used to develop realistic and achievable financial targets for the business.

Financial projections are presented in the form of tables, charts, and graphs within the business plan, providing a visual representation of the business's financial performance and trajectory. These projections are typically accompanied by a narrative explanation that outlines the key assumptions, methodologies, and drivers underlying the financial forecasts, and explains any significant variations or deviations from historical performance.

Financial projections provide a roadmap for the business's financial performance and growth, guiding strategic decision-making, resource allocation, and financial management. By developing realistic and achievable financial targets, gun stores and firearms-related businesses can effectively plan for the future, attract investors and lenders, and achieve long-term success in the competitive firearms market.

Location Selection and Store Layout

Location selection and store layout are crucial considerations for gun stores or firearms-related businesses, as they directly impact visibility, accessibility, customer traffic, and overall success. The process of selecting a location and designing the store layout involves careful analysis of various factors to ensure that the chosen location and layout effectively meet the needs of the business and its target customers.

Location selection begins with identifying potential locations that align with the business's target market, demographic profile, and operational requirements. Factors such as population density, demographics, proximity to shooting ranges, hunting areas, law enforcement facilities, and other complementary businesses are considered to determine the ideal location for the gun store.

Accessibility and visibility are key considerations when selecting a location, as the store should be easily accessible to customers and highly visible to passersby. High-traffic areas with good visibility, ample parking, and convenient access from major roads or highways are preferred to maximize exposure and attract customers.

Zoning regulations and local ordinances related to firearms sales and operations are carefully reviewed to ensure compliance and avoid potential legal issues. The chosen location should be in an area zoned for commercial or retail use and should comply with all relevant zoning regulations and ordinances governing firearms sales and operations.

Once a suitable location is identified, the store layout is designed to optimize space utilization, create an attractive and inviting atmosphere, and enhance the overall customer experience. The store layout is carefully planned to accommodate various functional areas, including retail display areas, product demonstration areas, customer service counters, checkout counters, storage areas, and office space.

The store layout is designed with customer flow in mind, ensuring that customers can easily navigate through the store and access products and services with minimal hassle. Clear signage, well-defined aisles, and strategic placement of merchandise help guide customers through the store and encourage exploration and engagement.

Merchandise displays are strategically positioned throughout the store to showcase products effectively and stimulate interest and impulse purchases. Firearms are displayed securely in glass cases or on racks with proper security measures in place to prevent theft and ensure customer safety.

Customer comfort and safety are prioritized in the store layout, with adequate lighting, comfortable seating areas, and clear signage indicating safety protocols and regulations. The layout is designed to facilitate safe handling of firearms and ensure compliance with all applicable safety standards and regulations.

The store layout is periodically reviewed and adjusted based on customer feedback, sales performance, and evolving business needs to optimize efficiency, enhance the customer experience, and drive sales.

Factors to Consider When Choosing a Location

When choosing a location for a gun store or firearms-related business, several factors should be considered to ensure the success and sustainability of the business. These factors include:

1. Zoning Regulations: Ensure that the chosen location complies with local zoning regulations governing firearms sales and operations. Check with local authorities to confirm that the chosen location is zoned appropriately for commercial or retail use and permits firearms-related businesses.

2. Accessibility: Choose a location that is easily accessible to customers, with ample parking and convenient access from major roads or highways. Consider factors such as proximity to main thoroughfares, public transportation options, and parking availability to ensure ease of access for customers.

3. Visibility: Select a location with high visibility to maximize exposure and attract customers. Choose a location with good visibility from major roads or highways, with signage that is easily visible and identifiable from a distance to draw attention to the business.

4. Target Market: Consider the demographic profile and preferences of the target market when selecting a location. Choose a location that is in close proximity to the target market, with demographics that align with the customer base of the business, such as firearm enthusiasts, hunters, sports shooters, or law enforcement personnel.

5. Competition: Evaluate the competitive landscape in the area to determine the level of competition from existing gun stores and firearms-related businesses. Choose a location that has limited direct competition or offers a unique advantage over competitors, such as a strategic location, unique product offerings, or superior customer service.

6. Safety and Security: Prioritize safety and security when selecting a location for a gun store. Choose a location in a safe and secure area with low crime rates and adequate security measures in place to protect the business, employees, and customers. Consider factors such as lighting, visibility, and proximity to law enforcement facilities when assessing safety and security.

7. Regulatory Compliance: Ensure that the chosen location complies with all federal, state, and local regulations governing firearms sales and operations. Consider factors such as licensing requirements, background check procedures, storage regulations, and zoning restrictions to ensure legal compliance and avoid potential legal issues.

8. Market Demand: Assess the demand for firearms and related products or services in the area when choosing a location. Conduct market research to determine the size and growth potential of the firearms market in the area, as well as customer preferences, purchasing behavior, and market trends.

9. Economic Factors: Consider economic factors such as population growth, income levels, employment rates, and consumer spending habits when selecting a location. Choose a location with a stable economy and favorable economic conditions that support business growth and sustainability.

10. Operational Considerations: Evaluate operational factors such as space requirements, lease terms, utility costs, and infrastructure availability when choosing a location. Consider factors such as the size and layout of the space, lease terms and conditions, utility costs, and access to essential services and amenities to ensure that the chosen location meets the operational needs of the business.

Considering these factors when choosing a location for a gun store or firearms-related business can help ensure that the selected location is well-suited to the needs of the business, maximizes visibility and accessibility, complies with regulatory requirements, and aligns with the preferences of the target market, ultimately contributing to the success and sustainability of the business.

Evaluating Demographics and Traffic Patterns

When evaluating demographics and traffic patterns for choosing a location, gun store owners need to consider various factors to ensure that the selected location aligns with their target market and provides ample opportunities for customer engagement and sales. Demographics play a crucial role in determining the suitability of a location, as they provide insights into the characteristics and preferences of the local population.

Gun store owners should assess the population density of the area surrounding potential locations. Areas with a higher population density typically offer a larger pool of potential customers and higher foot traffic, which can translate into increased visibility and sales opportunities for the business.

Additionally, analyzing the demographic composition of the local population is essential. Factors such as age, gender, income level, education level, occupation, and lifestyle preferences can influence purchasing behavior and preferences for firearms and related products. Understanding the demographics of the target market helps gun store owners tailor their product offerings and marketing strategies to effectively cater to the needs and preferences of local customers.

Another important consideration is the presence of target customer segments within the local population. Gun store owners should evaluate whether the demographics of the area align with their target customer segments, such as firearm enthusiasts, hunters, sports shooters, law enforcement personnel, and security professionals. Identifying areas with a higher concentration of target customers can help maximize the store's potential for attracting and retaining customers.

Analyzing traffic patterns and accessibility is also crucial when evaluating potential locations. Gun store owners should assess the volume and flow of pedestrian and vehicular traffic in the area, as well as the accessibility of the location from major roads, highways, and public transportation hubs. Locations with high foot traffic and easy access are more likely to attract customers and drive sales.

Evaluating the proximity of complementary businesses and amenities is important. Gun store owners should consider the presence of shooting ranges, hunting areas, law enforcement facilities, military bases, outdoor recreation areas, and other businesses that cater to firearms enthusiasts. Being located near such establishments can attract a steady stream of customers and enhance the overall appeal of the location.

Evaluating demographics and traffic patterns is essential for choosing a location that aligns with the target market and provides ample opportunities for customer engagement and sales. By carefully analyzing population density, demographic composition, target customer segments, traffic patterns, accessibility, and proximity to complementary businesses, gun store owners can make informed decisions and select a location that maximizes the potential for success in the competitive firearms market.

Designing an Effective Store Layout

Designing an effective store layout for a gun store or firearms-related business involves careful planning and consideration of various factors to create a functional, visually appealing, and customer-friendly environment. The store layout should be designed to optimize space utilization, enhance product visibility, facilitate customer navigation, and promote sales.

Here are key considerations when designing an effective store layout:

1. Traffic Flow: The layout should be designed to facilitate smooth traffic flow and guide customers through the store in a logical manner. Consider factors such as entrance and exit points, aisle width, and placement of displays to minimize congestion and make it easy for customers to navigate the store.

2. Product Placement: Arrange products strategically throughout the store to maximize visibility and encourage browsing. Place high-demand items and popular brands in prominent locations to attract attention and drive sales. Group related products together to make it easier for customers to find what they are looking for and encourage cross-selling.

3. Display Design: Use attractive and eye-catching displays to showcase products effectively. Utilize a combination of shelving, racks, display cases, and wall-mounted displays to create visually appealing product presentations. Ensure that products are displayed securely and safely, especially firearms, ammunition, and accessories.

4. Safety Considerations: Prioritize safety in the store layout by ensuring that firearms and ammunition are displayed and stored securely in compliance with regulatory requirements. Implement proper security measures such as locking display cases, security cameras, and alarm systems to prevent theft and ensure customer safety.

5. Customer Comfort: Create a comfortable and welcoming environment for customers by providing adequate lighting, comfortable seating areas, and clear signage. Ensure that aisles are wide enough to accommodate wheelchair accessibility and allow for easy navigation for all customers.

6. Checkout Area: Design the checkout area for efficiency and convenience. Position checkout counters near the entrance or exit to facilitate quick and easy transactions. Provide sufficient space for customers to queue comfortably and ensure that checkout staff have easy access to essential equipment and supplies.

7. Flexibility and Adaptability: Design the store layout with flexibility in mind to accommodate changes in inventory, seasonal promotions, and customer preferences. Use modular fixtures and adjustable displays that can be easily reconfigured to meet changing needs and optimize space utilization.

8. Branding and Merchandising: Incorporate branding elements and signage throughout the store to reinforce the business's identity and create a cohesive brand experience. Use effective merchandising techniques such as color coordination, product grouping, and signage to guide customer attention and promote featured products or promotions.

9. Accessibility: Ensure that the store layout is accessible to all customers, including those with disabilities. Provide clear signage and designated pathways for wheelchair access, and ensure that merchandise is displayed at accessible heights for customers of all heights and abilities.

10. Customer Feedback: Solicit feedback from customers to continuously improve the store layout and address any issues or concerns. Use customer feedback to identify areas for improvement and make adjustments to enhance the overall shopping experience.

Securing the Right Space and Negotiating Lease Terms

Securing the right space for a gun store or firearms-related business is a crucial step in establishing a successful retail location. It involves identifying suitable properties, assessing their suitability for the business's needs, and negotiating lease terms that are favorable and align with the business's objectives.

When searching for a retail space, gun store owners should consider factors such as location, size, layout, visibility, accessibility, zoning regulations, and proximity to target customers. The location should be strategically chosen to attract the target market and provide convenient access for customers. Consideration should also be given to factors such as parking availability, foot traffic, and neighboring businesses.

Once potential properties have been identified, thorough due diligence should be conducted to assess their suitability for the gun store. This includes inspecting the physical condition of the property, evaluating the layout and floor plan, assessing security measures, and considering any necessary renovations or modifications to accommodate the business's needs.

When negotiating lease terms, gun store owners should seek to secure favorable terms that support the long-term success of the business. This includes negotiating the lease duration, rental rate, rent escalation clauses, security deposit, tenant improvements, and other provisions that impact the cost and flexibility of the lease agreement.

It is important to carefully review and understand all lease terms and provisions before signing the lease agreement. Gun store owners should seek legal counsel to review the lease agreement and ensure that their rights and interests are protected. Attention should be given to clauses related to lease termination, renewal options, property maintenance and repairs, insurance requirements, and any restrictions or limitations that may impact the operation of the business.

Negotiating lease terms also involves advocating for provisions that provide flexibility and support the business's growth and success. This may include negotiating options to sublease or assign the lease, flexibility to make alterations or improvements to the space, and provisions that protect the business's ability to operate in compliance with regulatory requirements.

Effective negotiation skills are essential when securing the right space and negotiating lease terms for a gun store. Gun store owners should be prepared to articulate their needs and priorities, conduct market research to support their negotiation position, and engage in constructive dialogue with landlords or property managers to reach mutually beneficial lease terms.

Setting up Supplier Relationships

Setting up supplier relationships is a critical aspect of establishing a gun store or firearms-related business. Supplier relationships play a vital role in ensuring a reliable and consistent supply of firearms, ammunition, accessories, and other products essential for the operation of the business.

Here are key considerations when setting up supplier relationships:

Identifying Suppliers: Begin by researching and identifying potential suppliers of firearms, ammunition, accessories, and related products. This may include manufacturers, distributors, wholesalers, and importers specializing in firearms and shooting sports equipment. Consider factors such as product quality, pricing, availability, reliability, and reputation when evaluating potential suppliers.

Establishing Contact: Once potential suppliers have been identified, initiate contact to inquire about their products, pricing, terms, and conditions. Introduce your business and explain your requirements, including the types of products you are interested in, anticipated order volumes, and any specific needs or preferences.

Negotiating Terms: Negotiate terms and conditions with suppliers to establish a mutually beneficial relationship. This may include pricing, payment terms, order minimums, shipping terms, return policies, and any special arrangements or discounts available. Seek to negotiate terms that provide competitive pricing, favorable payment terms, and flexibility to accommodate the needs of your business.

Building Trust: Building trust and rapport with suppliers is essential for establishing long-term relationships. Communicate openly and transparently with suppliers, provide accurate and timely information about your business and product requirements, and fulfill your obligations as a customer. Establishing trust with suppliers helps foster a collaborative and mutually beneficial partnership.

Ensuring Compliance: Ensure that suppliers comply with all applicable laws, regulations, and industry standards related to the sale and distribution of firearms and related products. Verify that suppliers hold any necessary licenses, permits, or certifications required for their business operations, and confirm that their products meet all legal and safety requirements.

Managing Relationships: Actively manage relationships with suppliers to ensure smooth and efficient supply chain operations. Maintain open lines of communication with suppliers, address any issues or concerns promptly, and collaborate with suppliers to resolve problems and improve processes. Regularly review supplier performance and seek feedback to identify areas for improvement and opportunities for collaboration.

Diversifying Suppliers: Consider diversifying your supplier base to mitigate risks and ensure continuity of supply. Establish relationships with multiple suppliers to reduce dependence on any single supplier and provide flexibility to adapt to changes in market conditions or supplier availability. Diversifying suppliers also provides access to a broader range of products and pricing options.

Continuous Improvement: Continuously evaluate and improve supplier relationships to optimize supply chain performance and support business growth. Monitor market trends, evaluate supplier performance, and seek feedback from customers to identify opportunities for improvement and innovation in product selection, pricing, and service delivery.

Setting up supplier relationships is a strategic process that requires careful planning, negotiation, and management to establish reliable and mutually beneficial partnerships. By selecting reputable suppliers, negotiating favorable terms, building trust, ensuring compliance, managing relationships effectively, diversifying suppliers, and continuously improving supplier relationships, gun store owners can establish a robust supply chain that supports the success and growth of their business in the competitive firearms market.

Identifying Reliable Suppliers

Identifying reliable suppliers is essential for the success of a gun store or firearms-related business. Reliable suppliers ensure a consistent and high-quality supply of firearms, ammunition, accessories, and related products, which is crucial for meeting customer demand and maintaining business operations.

Here are key considerations when identifying reliable suppliers:

1. Reputation and Experience: Look for suppliers with a strong reputation and extensive experience in the firearms industry. Consider suppliers that have been in business for a significant period and have a track record of delivering high-quality products and reliable service to their customers. Check online reviews, testimonials, and industry references to gauge the reputation of potential suppliers.

2. Product Quality and Selection: Assess the quality and selection of products offered by potential suppliers. Look for suppliers that offer a wide range of firearms, ammunition, accessories, and related products from reputable brands and manufacturers. Evaluate the quality of products by requesting samples or inspecting product specifications, materials, and craftsmanship.

3. Compliance and Certification: Ensure that potential suppliers comply with all applicable laws, regulations, and industry standards governing the sale and distribution of firearms and related products. Verify that suppliers hold any necessary licenses, permits, or certifications required for their business operations, such as Federal Firearms License (FFL) or other relevant certifications.

4. Reliability and Consistency: Choose suppliers that demonstrate reliability and consistency in product availability, delivery times, and order fulfillment. Assess the supplier's track record for meeting deadlines, fulfilling orders accurately, and resolving any issues or discrepancies promptly. Consider suppliers with robust inventory management systems and logistical capabilities to ensure timely delivery of products.

5. Customer Service and Support: Evaluate the level of customer service and support provided by potential suppliers. Look for suppliers that offer responsive and personalized customer service, including timely communication, assistance with product selection, order tracking, and resolution of any issues or concerns. Choose suppliers that are committed to building strong relationships and providing ongoing support to their customers.

6. Pricing and Terms: Compare pricing and terms offered by potential suppliers to ensure competitiveness and affordability. Consider factors such as product pricing, shipping costs, payment terms, order minimums, and discounts available for bulk orders. Negotiate terms that align with your budget and business requirements while ensuring that pricing is competitive and transparent.

7. Supply Chain Transparency: Seek suppliers that provide transparency and visibility into their supply chain practices and sourcing methods. Choose suppliers that prioritize ethical sourcing, environmental sustainability, and compliance with industry standards and regulations. Request information about the supplier's manufacturing processes, sourcing practices, and commitment to responsible business practices.

8. References and Recommendations: Seek recommendations and references from industry peers, colleagues, or other trusted sources when identifying potential suppliers. Reach out to other gun store owners, shooting range operators, or industry associations for recommendations on reliable suppliers that they have worked with and trust.

Identifying reliable suppliers requires thorough research, due diligence, and careful evaluation of factors such as reputation, experience, product quality, compliance, reliability, customer service, pricing, and transparency. By selecting reputable suppliers that align with your business values and requirements, gun store owners can establish strong and sustainable partnerships that support the success and growth of their business in the competitive firearms market.

Establishing Vendor Relationships

Establishing vendor relationships is a crucial aspect of running a successful gun store or firearms-related business. These relationships ensure a steady and reliable supply of firearms, ammunition, accessories, and other essential products that are necessary for the operation of the business. Here are the key steps involved in establishing vendor relationships:

Research and Identify Potential Vendors: Begin by researching and identifying potential vendors who supply firearms, ammunition, accessories, and related products. This may include manufacturers, distributors, wholesalers, and importers specializing in firearms and shooting sports equipment. Utilize industry directories, trade shows, online marketplaces, and networking events to identify reputable vendors.

Contact Potential Vendors: Once potential vendors have been identified, reach out to them to inquire about their products, pricing, terms, and conditions. Introduce your business and explain your requirements, including the types of products you are interested in, anticipated order volumes, and any specific needs or preferences. Request product catalogs, price lists, and other relevant information to evaluate potential vendors.

Evaluate Vendor Credentials: Evaluate the credentials and reputation of potential vendors to ensure they are reliable and trustworthy partners. Consider factors such as industry experience, product quality, reliability, financial stability, customer service, and reputation within the firearms industry. Research vendor reviews, testimonials, and references from other businesses to gauge their track record and credibility.

Negotiate Terms and Conditions: Negotiate terms and conditions with vendors to establish a mutually beneficial relationship. This may include pricing, payment terms, order minimums, shipping terms, return policies, and any special arrangements or discounts available. Seek to negotiate terms that provide competitive pricing, favorable payment terms, and flexibility to accommodate the needs of your business.

Establish Open Communication: Maintain open lines of communication with vendors to facilitate effective collaboration and problem-solving. Establish a designated point of contact within your business to communicate with vendors and address any issues or concerns promptly. Communicate your expectations clearly and ensure that vendors are responsive and accessible when needed.

Place Initial Orders: Once terms have been negotiated and agreed upon, place initial orders with vendors to establish the business relationship. Start with smaller orders to test the reliability and quality of the products and services provided by vendors. Provide feedback to vendors based on your experience with their products and services to ensure continuous improvement and alignment with your business needs.

Build Long-Term Relationships: Focus on building long-term relationships with vendors based on trust, mutual respect, and collaboration. Foster a positive working relationship with vendors by honoring your commitments, paying invoices on time, providing timely feedback, and demonstrating professionalism in all interactions. Regularly review vendor performance and seek feedback to identify areas for improvement and opportunities for collaboration.

Monitor Vendor Performance: Monitor vendor performance regularly to ensure that they meet your expectations in terms of product quality, reliability, delivery times, and customer service. Keep track of key performance indicators such as order fulfillment rates, lead times, product availability, and customer satisfaction levels. Address any issues or concerns with vendors promptly to maintain a positive and productive relationship.

Negotiating Terms and Pricing

Negotiating terms and pricing with vendors is a critical aspect of establishing successful relationships that benefit both parties. Effective negotiation skills can help gun store owners secure favorable terms and pricing, ensuring competitive pricing for their products while maintaining profitability.

Here are key considerations when negotiating terms and pricing with vendors:

1. Preparation: Before entering into negotiations, conduct thorough research to understand market prices, industry trends, and competitors' pricing strategies. Determine your desired pricing objectives and the maximum budget you are willing to allocate for product purchases. Gather information about the vendor's pricing structure, terms, and conditions to identify areas for negotiation.

2. Define Objectives: Clearly define your objectives and priorities for the negotiation process. Determine the specific terms and pricing points you aim to negotiate, such as unit pricing, volume discounts, payment terms, shipping costs, return policies, and any other relevant terms that impact the overall cost and profitability of the transaction.

3. Establish Relationships: Build rapport and establish positive relationships with vendors before engaging in negotiations. Emphasize the importance of a mutually beneficial partnership and demonstrate professionalism and respect in all interactions. Building trust and rapport with vendors can create a conducive environment for constructive negotiations and facilitate the achievement of mutually acceptable terms.

4. Communicate Value: Clearly articulate the value proposition of your business to the vendor during negotiations. Highlight your purchasing power, order volume, and potential for repeat business to leverage negotiating leverage. Emphasize the benefits of establishing a long-term partnership, such as reliability, stability, and predictability of orders.

5. Identify Areas for Negotiation: Identify specific areas for negotiation based on your objectives and priorities. This may include negotiating pricing discounts based on volume purchases, securing favorable payment terms (e.g., extended payment terms, early payment discounts), negotiating shipping costs or terms, and discussing incentives or promotions offered by the vendor.

6. Present Proposals: Present your negotiation proposals to the vendor clearly and confidently, supported by relevant data and rationale. Justify your proposed terms and pricing based on market research, industry benchmarks, and the value provided by your business. Be prepared to discuss and negotiate alternative solutions or compromises to reach mutually acceptable terms.

7. Listen and Collaborate: Actively listen to the vendor's perspective and concerns during negotiations. Collaborate with the vendor to explore potential solutions that address both parties' needs and interests. Be open to compromise and flexible in finding creative solutions that benefit both parties and contribute to the success of the partnership.

8. Document Agreements: Once negotiations are finalized, document the agreed-upon terms and pricing in a written contract or purchase agreement. Ensure that all terms, pricing, and conditions are clearly outlined in the agreement to avoid misunderstandings or disputes in the future. Review the contract carefully with legal counsel before signing to ensure that your interests are protected.

9. Maintain Relationships: After reaching an agreement, maintain open lines of communication with the vendor and nurture the relationship over time. Honor your commitments, pay invoices on time, and provide feedback on product quality and service levels to foster a positive and productive partnership.

10. Monitor and Review: Continuously monitor vendor performance and review the terms and pricing periodically to ensure that they remain competitive and aligned with your business objectives. Address any issues or concerns with vendors promptly and collaborate on solutions to maintain a positive and mutually beneficial relationship.

Developing a Inventory Management Strategy

Developing an inventory management strategy is essential for gun stores or firearms-related businesses to effectively manage their inventory levels, optimize stock availability, minimize stock-outs, reduce excess inventory, and maximize profitability. A well-designed inventory management strategy ensures that the right products are available at the right time, in the right quantities, to meet customer demand while minimizing costs and maximizing efficiency.

Here's how to develop an effective inventory management strategy:

1. Inventory Analysis: Start by conducting a thorough analysis of your current inventory levels, sales history, and product performance. Identify fast-moving items, slow-moving items, seasonal trends, and obsolete or discontinued products. Analyze historical sales data to forecast future demand and identify patterns and trends that can inform your inventory management decisions.

2. Inventory Classification: Classify your inventory into categories based on factors such as demand variability, sales velocity, and profitability. Use techniques such as ABC analysis to prioritize inventory items into categories (A, B, C) based on their importance and contribution to sales and profitability. This allows you to focus your attention and resources on managing high-value and high-demand items more effectively.

3. Setting Reorder Points and Safety Stock Levels: Establish reorder points and safety stock levels for each inventory item based on demand forecasts, lead times, and service level targets. Reorder points indicate when to reorder inventory to replenish stock levels, while safety stock levels provide a buffer to protect against unexpected fluctuations in demand or delays in supplier deliveries. Set reorder points and safety stock levels based on factors such as lead times, demand variability, and desired service levels to ensure optimal inventory levels while minimizing stock-outs and excess inventory.

4. **Vendor Management:** Establish strong relationships with suppliers and vendors to ensure reliable and timely supply of inventory. Negotiate favorable terms and pricing with vendors to optimize purchasing costs and minimize lead times. Monitor vendor performance regularly and address any issues or concerns promptly to ensure smooth supply chain operations.

5. **Inventory Tracking and Monitoring:** Implement inventory tracking and monitoring systems to accurately track inventory levels, sales, and stock movements in real-time. Use inventory management software or systems to automate inventory tracking, monitor stock levels, and generate reports on inventory performance. Regularly reconcile physical inventory counts with system records to identify discrepancies and ensure accurate inventory records.

6. **Just-in-Time (JIT) Inventory:** Consider adopting a just-in-time (JIT) inventory management approach to minimize carrying costs and optimize inventory levels. JIT inventory systems involve ordering inventory from suppliers only when needed, based on actual customer demand, rather than maintaining large stockpiles of inventory. This helps reduce carrying costs, minimize excess inventory, and improve cash flow by reducing the amount of capital tied up in inventory.

7. Inventory Turnover and Days' Sales of Inventory (DSI): Monitor inventory turnover and days' sales of inventory (DSI) to assess the efficiency of your inventory management practices. Inventory turnover measures how quickly inventory is sold and replaced within a given period, while DSI measures the number of days it takes for inventory to be sold. Aim to achieve a balance between maximizing inventory turnover to minimize carrying costs and maintaining sufficient inventory levels to meet customer demand.

8. Demand Forecasting and Planning: Utilize demand forecasting techniques to predict future demand for inventory items and plan inventory levels accordingly. Use historical sales data, market trends, seasonal factors, and other relevant data to develop accurate demand forecasts and plan inventory levels to meet anticipated demand while minimizing excess inventory and stock-outs.

9. Continuous Improvement: Continuously monitor and evaluate your inventory management practices to identify opportunities for improvement. Analyze inventory performance metrics, such as inventory turnover, stock-out rates, and carrying costs, and implement changes to optimize inventory levels, streamline processes, and improve overall efficiency and profitability.

10. Collaboration Across Departments: Foster collaboration and communication across departments, such as sales, purchasing, and operations, to ensure alignment and coordination in inventory management efforts. Involve key stakeholders in decision-making processes and leverage cross-functional expertise to develop and implement effective inventory management strategies that support the overall goals and objectives of the business.

developing a comprehensive inventory management strategy that addresses key aspects such as inventory analysis, classification, reorder points, safety stock levels, vendor management, inventory tracking, JIT inventory, demand forecasting, continuous improvement, and collaboration across departments, gun stores and firearms-related businesses can optimize inventory levels, improve operational efficiency, and maximize profitability in the competitive firearms market.

Store Operations and Security

Store operations and security are critical aspects of running a successful gun store or firearms-related business. These areas encompass various processes, procedures, and measures designed to ensure the smooth and secure operation of the store while adhering to regulatory requirements and maintaining a safe environment for customers and staff. Here's a detailed overview of store operations and security:

Store Operations:

1. Opening and Closing Procedures: Establish clear opening and closing procedures to ensure the store is properly prepared for business hours and securely closed at the end of the day. This includes tasks such as checking inventory levels, verifying cash registers, arming security systems, and securing firearms and valuables.

2. Customer Service: Provide excellent customer service to enhance the overall shopping experience for customers. Train staff to greet customers warmly, assist with product inquiries, provide product

demonstrations, and offer knowledgeable advice and guidance on firearms and related products.

3. Sales Processes: Implement efficient sales processes to facilitate transactions and ensure compliance with regulatory requirements. Train staff on proper sales procedures, including background checks, identification verification, completion of paperwork, and adherence to waiting periods and other legal requirements for firearm purchases.

4. Inventory Management: Maintain accurate inventory records and implement effective inventory management practices to ensure optimal stock levels, minimize stock-outs and excess inventory, and streamline inventory replenishment processes. Utilize inventory management software or systems to track stock levels, monitor product movements, and generate reports on inventory performance.

5. Merchandising and Displays: Design attractive and well-organized merchandise displays to showcase products effectively and stimulate customer interest. Rotate merchandise regularly to keep displays fresh and engaging, and highlight featured products or promotions to drive sales.

6. Cleaning and Maintenance: Implement regular cleaning and maintenance schedules to keep the store clean, organized, and visually appealing. Clean and maintain display cases, shelves,

floors, and other surfaces to create a welcoming environment for customers and ensure product visibility.

7. Training and Development: Provide ongoing training and development opportunities for staff to enhance their skills, product knowledge, and customer service abilities. Conduct regular training sessions on topics such as firearm safety, regulatory compliance, customer service best practices, and sales techniques to ensure staff are well-equipped to perform their roles effectively.

Store Security:

1. Physical Security Measures: Implement physical security measures to protect the store, inventory, and personnel from unauthorized access, theft, and vandalism. This may include installing security cameras, alarm systems, motion sensors, and access control measures to monitor and control access to the premises.

2. Firearm Security: Implement strict security protocols for handling and storing firearms to prevent unauthorized access and ensure compliance with regulatory requirements. Secure firearms in locked display cases or safes, and implement additional security measures such as trigger locks and cable locks to prevent unauthorized use or theft.

3. Cash Handling Procedures: Establish secure cash handling procedures to minimize the risk of theft and ensure the safe handling of cash transactions. This may include using secure cash registers, conducting regular cash reconciliations, and implementing protocols for depositing cash in safes or bank accounts.

4. Employee Security Training: Provide security training for staff to educate them on security protocols, emergency procedures, and measures to prevent theft and unauthorized access. Train staff to identify suspicious behavior, handle security incidents appropriately, and respond to emergency situations effectively.

5. Regulatory Compliance: Ensure compliance with all relevant federal, state, and local regulations governing firearms sales and security requirements. Stay updated on changes to regulations and implement necessary measures to ensure compliance with background check procedures, waiting periods, record-keeping requirements, and other legal obligations.

6. Incident Response Plan: Develop an incident response plan to address security breaches, emergencies, or other incidents that may occur in the store. Establish protocols for responding to security alarms, reporting incidents to authorities, and implementing emergency procedures to ensure the safety of customers and staff.

7. Security Audits and Reviews: Conduct regular security audits and reviews to assess the effectiveness of security measures and identify areas for improvement. Review security camera footage, analyze security incidents, and solicit feedback from staff to evaluate the security posture of the store and implement enhancements as needed.

Effective store operations and security measures are essential for ensuring the smooth and secure operation of a gun store or firearms-related business. By implementing robust operational processes, providing excellent customer service, maintaining strict security measures, and ensuring compliance with regulatory requirements, gun store owners can create a safe and welcoming environment for customers while protecting the store, inventory, and personnel from security threats and risks.

Hiring and Training Staff

Hiring and training staff are critical components of running a successful gun store or firearms-related business. The process involves recruiting, selecting, onboarding, and training qualified individuals who are capable of providing excellent customer service, adhering to regulatory requirements, and upholding the values and standards of the business.

Here's a detailed overview of hiring and training staff:

1. Recruitment: Begin by identifying the staffing needs of the business and developing job descriptions outlining the roles and responsibilities of each position. Advertise job openings through various channels, such as online job boards, industry associations, social media, and local newspapers, to attract qualified candidates. Screen resumes, conduct interviews, and assess candidates' qualifications, experience, and suitability for the role.

2. Selection: Select candidates who possess the necessary skills, experience, and qualifications to perform the job effectively. Evaluate candidates based on criteria such as interpersonal skills, communication abilities, customer service orientation, product knowledge, and familiarity with firearms and shooting sports. Consider factors such as cultural fit, reliability, and availability when making hiring decisions.

3. Onboarding: Once candidates have been selected, facilitate a comprehensive onboarding process to introduce new hires to the business, its policies, procedures, and expectations. Provide an overview of the business's mission, vision, values, and organizational structure. Familiarize new hires with their roles and responsibilities, and provide training on essential job functions, including customer service, sales techniques, regulatory compliance, and firearm safety protocols.

4. Training: Develop and implement a structured training program to equip staff with the knowledge, skills, and competencies required to perform their roles effectively. Provide training on firearm safety, product knowledge, customer service best practices, sales techniques, regulatory requirements, and store policies and procedures. Incorporate hands-on training, role-playing exercises, and shadowing opportunities to enhance learning and skill development.

5. Ongoing Development: Support staff development and continuous learning by providing opportunities for ongoing training and skill development. Offer access to industry-related training programs, certification courses, workshops, and seminars to enhance staff knowledge and expertise. Encourage staff to pursue professional development opportunities and acquire additional certifications or qualifications relevant to their roles.

6. Performance Management: Establish performance management processes to monitor and evaluate staff performance regularly. Set clear performance expectations and goals for each employee, and provide regular feedback and coaching to support their development and improvement. Conduct performance reviews periodically to assess progress, identify strengths and areas for improvement, and align performance with organizational objectives.

7. Team Building: Foster a positive work environment and promote teamwork and collaboration among staff members. Organize team-building activities, staff meetings, and social events to strengthen relationships, boost morale, and enhance communication and camaraderie among team members. Encourage open communication, mutual respect, and a supportive team culture within the workplace.

8. Leadership Development: Identify potential leaders within the organization and provide opportunities for leadership development and advancement. Offer leadership training programs, mentorship opportunities, and career development paths to cultivate leadership skills and groom future leaders within the organization. Invest in the growth and development of staff members to build a strong leadership pipeline and support succession planning efforts.

9. Compliance and Safety Training: Ensure that staff receive comprehensive training on regulatory compliance and safety protocols related to firearms sales and operations. Provide training on background check procedures, identification verification, firearm safety rules, safe handling practices, and emergency response procedures. Emphasize the importance of adhering to legal requirements and maintaining a safe environment for customers and staff.

10. Employee Engagement: Foster a culture of employee engagement and empowerment by soliciting feedback, recognizing and rewarding performance, and involving staff in decision-making processes. Encourage open communication, listen to employee concerns, and address issues promptly to foster a positive work environment and enhance staff morale and satisfaction.

Hiring and training staff are essential processes for building a competent and engaged workforce that contributes to the success and growth of a gun store or firearms-related business. By recruiting qualified candidates, providing comprehensive training and development opportunities, fostering a supportive work environment, and promoting continuous learning and improvement, gun store owners can build a strong team capable of delivering exceptional customer service, ensuring regulatory compliance, and driving business success.

Implementing Inventory Management Systems

Implementing inventory management systems is crucial for gun stores or firearms-related businesses to effectively manage their inventory levels, streamline operations, optimize stock availability, and maximize profitability. An inventory management system is a software solution designed to track inventory levels, monitor stock movements, automate inventory-related tasks, and generate reports to support decision-making.

Here's a detailed overview of implementing inventory management systems:

1. Needs Assessment: Begin by conducting a thorough needs assessment to identify the specific requirements and challenges related to inventory management in your gun store. Consider factors such as the size of your inventory, the complexity of your product catalog, the frequency of inventory turnover, and any unique regulatory requirements related to firearms sales.

2. Research and Selection: Research available inventory management software solutions and select a system that best aligns with your business needs, budget, and operational requirements. Evaluate factors such as features and functionalities, scalability, ease of use, integration capabilities, customer support, and pricing options. Request product demonstrations, trial periods, or references from software vendors to assess the suitability of the system for your business.

3. System Customization: Work with the software vendor to customize the inventory management system to meet your specific needs and preferences. Configure the system settings, workflows, and user permissions to align with your business processes and organizational structure. Customize data fields, product attributes, and reporting options to capture relevant information and generate actionable insights for inventory management.

4. Data Migration: Transfer existing inventory data and product information from legacy systems, spreadsheets, or manual records to the new inventory management system. Ensure that data is accurately imported, validated, and mapped to the corresponding fields in the new system to maintain data integrity and consistency.

5. Staff Training: Provide comprehensive training for staff on how to use the inventory management system effectively. Train employees on system functionalities, navigation, data entry procedures, and best practices for inventory management. Offer hands-on training sessions, user manuals, and online resources to support staff learning and adoption of the new system.

6. Integration with Existing Systems: Integrate the inventory management system with other existing systems, such as point-of-sale (POS) systems, accounting software, e-commerce platforms, and supplier portals, to streamline data exchange and improve operational efficiency. Ensure seamless integration between systems to facilitate accurate inventory tracking, order processing, and financial reporting.

7. Implementation Timeline: Develop a detailed implementation plan with clear timelines, milestones, and responsibilities to guide the implementation process. Define key milestones for system setup, data migration, staff training, and system testing to ensure a smooth and successful implementation. Allocate sufficient time and resources for each phase of the implementation process and closely monitor progress to ensure timely completion.

8. Testing and Quality Assurance: Conduct thorough testing and quality assurance checks to validate the functionality and performance of the inventory management system. Test system workflows, data accuracy, reporting capabilities, and integration points to identify any issues or discrepancies. Address any identified issues promptly and conduct additional testing as needed to ensure system reliability and accuracy.

9. Go-Live and Transition: Plan and execute a smooth transition to the new inventory management system. Coordinate with staff to schedule the system go-live date and ensure adequate support and resources are available during the transition period. Communicate changes and updates to staff, suppliers, and other stakeholders, and provide ongoing support and assistance to address any issues or concerns during the transition.

10. Continuous Improvement: Continuously monitor and evaluate the performance of the inventory management system to identify opportunities for improvement and optimization. Gather feedback from staff and stakeholders on system usability, functionality, and effectiveness, and implement enhancements or updates as needed to address evolving business needs and improve system performance.

Ensuring Compliance with Security Measures

Ensuring compliance with security measures is a critical aspect of running a gun store or firearms-related business to protect the store, inventory, and personnel from security threats, theft, and regulatory violations. Compliance with security measures involves implementing and maintaining a comprehensive security program that aligns with regulatory requirements, industry best practices, and the unique security needs of the business.

Here's a detailed overview of ensuring compliance with security measures:

1. Regulatory Compliance: Stay updated on federal, state, and local regulations governing firearms sales, security requirements, and safety standards. Familiarize yourself with relevant laws, regulations, and guidelines issued by regulatory authorities such as the Bureau of Alcohol, Tobacco, Firearms, and Explosives (ATF), as well as state and local law enforcement agencies. Ensure compliance with background check procedures, waiting periods, record-keeping requirements, and other legal obligations related to firearms sales and security.

2. Physical Security Measures: Implement physical security measures to protect the store, inventory, and personnel from unauthorized access, theft, and vandalism. Install security cameras,

alarm systems, motion sensors, and access control measures to monitor and control access to the premises. Secure entry points, windows, and doors with sturdy locks and reinforced barriers to deter intruders and unauthorized entry. Ensure that firearms and valuables are stored securely in locked display cases, safes, or vaults to prevent theft and unauthorized access.

3. Firearm Security: Implement strict security protocols for handling and storing firearms to prevent unauthorized access and ensure compliance with regulatory requirements. Secure firearms in locked display cases or safes equipped with tamper-resistant locks and alarm systems. Implement additional security measures such as trigger locks, cable locks, and firearm tethering devices to prevent unauthorized use or theft. Conduct regular inventory audits and reconcile inventory records to ensure accurate tracking and accountability of firearms.

4. Cash Handling Procedures: Establish secure cash handling procedures to minimize the risk of theft and ensure the safe handling of cash transactions. Use secure cash registers equipped with cash drawers, locking mechanisms, and counterfeit detection features. Implement protocols for cash management, including cash reconciliation, deposits, and withdrawals, to minimize the risk of cash loss or discrepancies. Train staff on proper cash handling procedures and security measures to mitigate the risk of theft or loss.

5. Employee Security Training: Provide security training for staff to educate them on security protocols, emergency procedures, and measures to prevent theft and unauthorized access. Train staff to identify suspicious behavior, handle security incidents appropriately, and respond to emergency situations effectively. Conduct regular security awareness training sessions to reinforce security practices and ensure that staff remain vigilant and alert to potential security threats.

6. Visitor Management: Implement visitor management protocols to control and monitor access to the premises and ensure the safety and security of the store environment. Require visitors to sign in and provide identification upon entry, and issue visitor badges or passes to identify authorized individuals. Escort visitors to designated areas and supervise their activities while on the premises to prevent unauthorized access to restricted areas or sensitive areas such as firearm storage areas.

7. Incident Response Plan: Develop an incident response plan to address security breaches, emergencies, or other incidents that may occur in the store. Establish protocols for responding to security alarms, reporting incidents to authorities, and implementing emergency procedures to ensure the safety of customers and staff. Conduct regular drills and exercises to test the effectiveness of the

incident response plan and train staff on their roles and responsibilities during emergencies.

8. Security Audits and Reviews: Conduct regular security audits and reviews to assess the effectiveness of security measures and identify areas for improvement. Review security camera footage, analyze security incidents, and conduct physical inspections to evaluate the security posture of the store and identify vulnerabilities or weaknesses. Implement corrective actions and enhancements based on the findings of security audits to strengthen security measures and mitigate security risks.

9. Collaboration with Law Enforcement: Collaborate with local law enforcement agencies to enhance security measures and address security concerns effectively. Establish relationships with law enforcement authorities and engage in proactive communication and collaboration to share information, report suspicious activities, and seek assistance in responding to security incidents or emergencies. Work with law enforcement agencies to conduct joint security assessments, training exercises, and crime prevention initiatives to enhance the overall security of the store and surrounding community.

10. Continuous Improvement: Continuously monitor and evaluate the effectiveness of security measures and make adjustments as needed to enhance security and ensure compliance with regulatory

requirements. Stay updated on emerging security threats, industry trends, and best practices in security management to proactively address evolving security risks. Engage staff and stakeholders in ongoing discussions and initiatives to promote a culture of security awareness and vigilance within the organization.

Managing Day-to-Day Operations

Managing day-to-day operations in a gun store or firearms-related business involves overseeing a wide range of activities to ensure the smooth and efficient functioning of the business. This includes managing inventory, sales, customer service, staff, security, and compliance with regulatory requirements.

Here's a detailed overview of managing day-to-day operations:

Inventory Management: Supervise inventory levels, track stock movements, and monitor product availability to ensure optimal inventory levels and minimize stock-outs or excess inventory. Implement inventory management processes to accurately track inventory, conduct regular inventory audits, and replenish stock as needed to meet customer demand.

Sales Operations: Oversee sales activities, monitor sales performance, and ensure that sales targets are met. Train sales staff on product knowledge, sales techniques, and customer service best practices to maximize sales opportunities and enhance customer satisfaction. Implement sales strategies, promotions, and incentives to drive sales and increase revenue.

Customer Service: Provide excellent customer service to enhance the overall shopping experience for customers. Train staff to greet customers warmly, assist with product inquiries, provide product demonstrations, and offer knowledgeable advice and guidance on firearms and related products. Address customer concerns and resolve issues promptly to ensure customer satisfaction and loyalty.

Staff Management: Manage staffing levels, schedules, and assignments to ensure adequate coverage and efficient operation of the store. Supervise staff performance, provide feedback, and coach employees to improve performance and enhance productivity. Conduct staff meetings, training sessions, and performance reviews to foster a positive work environment and promote employee engagement and development.

Security Management: Implement and enforce security measures to protect the store, inventory, and personnel from security threats, theft, and regulatory violations. Monitor security systems, conduct regular security audits, and enforce compliance with security protocols and procedures. Train staff on security awareness, emergency response procedures, and measures to prevent theft and unauthorized access.

Regulatory Compliance: Ensure compliance with federal, state, and local regulations governing firearms sales, security requirements, and safety standards. Stay updated on regulatory changes, maintain accurate records, and implement procedures to ensure compliance with background check procedures, waiting periods, record-keeping requirements, and other legal obligations related to firearms sales and operations.

Financial Management: Monitor financial performance, manage expenses, and ensure that the business operates within budgetary constraints. Review financial reports, analyze sales data, and identify opportunities to improve profitability and operational efficiency. Implement cost-saving measures, negotiate vendor contracts, and optimize pricing strategies to maximize revenue and minimize expenses.

Marketing and Promotion: Develop and implement marketing strategies and promotional activities to attract customers and drive sales. Utilize various marketing channels, such as digital marketing, social media, email marketing, and traditional advertising, to promote products, special offers, and events. Monitor marketing campaigns, track performance metrics, and adjust strategies as needed to optimize results and reach target audiences.

Operational Efficiency: Identify opportunities to improve operational efficiency and streamline processes to enhance productivity and reduce costs. Implement automation tools, technology solutions, and process improvements to streamline inventory management, sales operations, and administrative tasks. Monitor key performance indicators, analyze operational data, and implement changes to optimize workflow and resource allocation.

Continuous Improvement: Continuously evaluate and improve day-to-day operations to enhance business performance and customer satisfaction. Seek feedback from customers, staff, and stakeholders to identify areas for improvement and implement initiatives to address feedback and suggestions. Stay updated on industry trends, best practices, and emerging technologies to remain competitive and drive continuous improvement in day-to-day operations.

Marketing and Promotions

Marketing and promotions play a crucial role in promoting a gun store or firearms-related business, attracting customers, and driving sales. Effective marketing strategies and promotional activities help to increase brand awareness, generate leads, and engage customers to grow the business.

Here's a detailed overview of marketing and promotions for a gun store:

1. Branding: Develop a strong and distinctive brand identity that reflects the values, mission, and unique offerings of the gun store. Create a memorable logo, brand colors, and visual elements that resonate with the target audience and differentiate the business from competitors.

2. Target Audience: Identify and understand the target audience for the gun store, including demographics, interests, behaviors, and preferences. Tailor marketing messages, promotions, and campaigns to resonate with the needs and interests of the target audience.

3. Digital Marketing: Utilize digital marketing channels to reach and engage potential customers online. Develop a professional website that showcases products, services, and store information. Implement search engine optimization (SEO) strategies to improve the visibility of the website in search engine results. Utilize social media platforms such as Facebook, Instagram, and Twitter to share content, interact with customers, and promote products and promotions.

4. Email Marketing: Implement email marketing campaigns to communicate with customers, promote products, and drive sales. Build an email subscriber list by offering incentives such as discounts or special offers for signing up. Send regular newsletters, product updates, and promotional emails to keep customers informed and engaged.

5. Content Marketing: Create valuable and informative content related to firearms, shooting sports, and outdoor activities to attract and engage customers. Develop blog posts, articles, videos, and infographics that provide useful tips, advice, and insights for firearms enthusiasts. Share content on the website, social media, and other digital channels to position the gun store as a trusted resource and authority in the industry.

6. Events and Promotions: Host events, promotions, and special offers to attract customers and drive foot traffic to the store. Organize product demonstrations, shooting range events, or training workshops to showcase products and provide hands-on experiences for customers. Offer promotions such as discounts, sales, or exclusive offers to incentivize purchases and increase sales.

7. Local Marketing: Implement local marketing strategies to target customers in the local community and surrounding areas. Partner with local shooting ranges, gun clubs, and outdoor organizations to promote the gun store and reach potential customers. Sponsor local events, participate in community activities, and advertise in local publications to increase brand visibility and attract local customers.

8. Customer Loyalty Programs: Implement customer loyalty programs to reward repeat customers and encourage customer retention. Offer rewards such as discounts, freebies, or exclusive offers for loyal customers who make repeat purchases or refer new customers to the store. Create a loyalty program that incentivizes customers to return to the store and build long-term relationships with the brand.

9. Online Reviews and Testimonials: Encourage satisfied customers to leave positive reviews and testimonials online to build trust and credibility for the gun store. Monitor online review platforms such as Google My Business, Yelp, and Facebook for customer feedback

and respond promptly to reviews to demonstrate customer care and address any concerns or issues raised by customers.

10. Measurement and Analysis: Track and measure the effectiveness of marketing campaigns and promotions to evaluate performance and make data-driven decisions. Utilize analytics tools and metrics such as website traffic, social media engagement, email open rates, and sales data to assess the impact of marketing efforts and identify areas for improvement. Adjust marketing strategies and tactics based on performance insights to optimize results and drive business growth.

Developing a Marketing Plan

Developing a marketing plan for a gun store or firearms-related business involves creating a strategic roadmap to promote products, attract customers, and drive sales. A well-crafted marketing plan outlines the objectives, target audience, marketing strategies, tactics, and budget allocation to achieve business goals.

Here's a detailed overview of developing a marketing plan:

Understanding Business Goals: Start by identifying the overarching business goals and objectives that the marketing plan aims to support. These goals may include increasing sales revenue, expanding market reach, enhancing brand awareness, or launching new products or services. Align marketing objectives with broader business objectives to ensure that marketing efforts contribute to the overall success of the business.

Target Audience Analysis: Conduct thorough research to understand the target audience for the gun store, including demographics, interests, behaviors, and preferences. Segment the target audience into distinct groups based on factors such as age, gender, location, interests, and purchasing behavior. Develop detailed buyer personas that represent ideal customers to tailor marketing messages and strategies to resonate with the needs and preferences of the target audience.

SWOT Analysis: Perform a SWOT (Strengths, Weaknesses, Opportunities, Threats) analysis to assess the internal strengths and weaknesses of the gun store, as well as external opportunities and threats in the market. Identify key strengths to leverage in marketing efforts, address weaknesses that may impact marketing effectiveness, capitalize on opportunities to grow the business, and mitigate threats that may pose challenges to marketing success.

Setting Marketing Objectives: Define specific, measurable, achievable, relevant, and time-bound (SMART) marketing objectives that align with business goals and target audience needs. Examples of marketing objectives may include increasing website traffic, improving social media engagement, generating leads, boosting sales revenue, or enhancing brand visibility. Ensure that marketing objectives are realistic and attainable within the specified timeframe.

Marketing Strategies: Develop overarching marketing strategies that outline the approach and tactics for achieving marketing objectives. Consider various marketing channels, tactics, and techniques to reach and engage the target audience effectively. Common marketing strategies for gun stores may include digital marketing, social media marketing, content marketing, email marketing, local marketing, event marketing, and customer relationship management (CRM) strategies.

Tactical Execution: Outline specific marketing tactics and activities to implement each marketing strategy. Determine the timing, frequency, and sequence of marketing activities to maximize impact and effectiveness. Develop a detailed marketing calendar or schedule to plan and organize marketing initiatives, promotions, campaigns, and events throughout the year. Assign responsibilities and allocate resources for executing marketing tactics and activities.

Budget Allocation: Allocate a budget for implementing the marketing plan based on available resources, business priorities, and expected return on investment (ROI). Determine the appropriate budget allocation for each marketing strategy and tactic, considering factors such as advertising costs, promotional expenses, personnel costs, technology investments, and other marketing-related expenses. Monitor and track marketing expenditures to ensure that spending aligns with budgetary constraints and delivers measurable results.

Measurement and Evaluation: Establish key performance indicators (KPIs) and metrics to measure the effectiveness and success of marketing efforts. Track and monitor relevant metrics such as website traffic, social media engagement, email open rates, lead generation, conversion rates, sales revenue, customer acquisition cost (CAC), and return on investment (ROI). Analyze performance data regularly to evaluate marketing performance, identify areas for improvement, and make data-driven decisions to optimize marketing strategies and tactics.

Adjustment and Optimization: Continuously evaluate the performance of the marketing plan and make adjustments as needed to optimize results and achieve marketing objectives. Monitor market trends, consumer behavior, and competitive landscape to adapt marketing strategies and tactics accordingly. Test and experiment with different marketing approaches, messaging variations, and creative elements to identify what resonates most with the target audience. Use performance insights and feedback to refine marketing strategies, reallocate resources, and optimize marketing efforts for maximum effectiveness and impact.

Creating a Strong Brand Identity

Creating a strong brand identity is essential for a gun store or firearms-related business to differentiate itself from competitors, build credibility, and establish a memorable presence in the market. A strong brand identity reflects the values, personality, and unique offerings of the business, resonating with customers and fostering loyalty.

Here's a detailed overview of creating a strong brand identity:

1. Define Brand Values and Mission: Start by defining the core values and mission of the gun store. Identify the principles, beliefs, and ideals that the brand stands for and align them with the needs and aspirations of the target audience. Articulate a clear and compelling mission statement that communicates the purpose and vision of the business, guiding its actions and decisions.

2. Identify Target Audience: Understand the target audience for the gun store, including demographics, interests, behaviors, and preferences. Develop detailed buyer personas that represent ideal customers, taking into account factors such as age, gender, location, lifestyle, and purchasing behavior. Tailor the brand identity to resonate with the needs and preferences of the target audience, creating a strong connection and relevance.

3. Craft Brand Personality: Define the personality and character of the brand, conveying its unique traits, tone, and style. Determine whether the brand identity is bold and adventurous, professional and authoritative, friendly and approachable, or innovative and cutting-edge. Consistently express the brand personality across all brand touchpoints, including logo design, visual elements, messaging, and customer interactions.

4. Design Visual Identity: Develop a visually appealing and cohesive brand identity that reflects the personality and values of the gun store. Create a distinctive logo that symbolizes the brand and resonates with the target audience. Choose brand colors, typography, and graphic elements that convey the desired brand image and evoke the intended emotions. Ensure consistency in visual elements across all brand materials, including signage, packaging, website, and marketing collateral.

5. Establish Brand Voice: Define the brand voice and tone that will be used in communication with customers and stakeholders. Determine whether the brand voice is formal and professional, casual and conversational, or authoritative and informative. Develop brand messaging guidelines that outline the tone, style, and language to be used in written and verbal communication, ensuring consistency and clarity in brand communication.

6. Create Brand Story: Craft a compelling brand story that articulates the history, values, and unique selling proposition of the gun store. Share the story of how the business was founded, its mission and values, and what sets it apart from competitors. Incorporate storytelling into brand communication to create emotional connections with customers, humanize the brand, and build trust and loyalty.

7. Develop Brand Experience: Create a memorable and consistent brand experience for customers across all touchpoints and interactions with the gun store. Ensure that the brand identity is reflected in every aspect of the customer experience, from the store environment and product packaging to customer service interactions and online presence. Deliver exceptional customer experiences that align with the brand values and reinforce its identity.

8. Build Brand Consistency: Maintain consistency in brand identity across all marketing channels, platforms, and touchpoints to build brand recognition and trust. Establish brand guidelines that define the standards and specifications for using brand elements, including logo usage, colors, typography, imagery, and messaging. Ensure that all employees, partners, and stakeholders understand and adhere to brand guidelines to maintain brand consistency.

9. Engage with Customers: Foster engagement and interaction with customers to strengthen the brand identity and build brand loyalty. Encourage customer feedback, reviews, and testimonials to demonstrate the value and credibility of the brand. Engage with customers on social media, respond to inquiries and comments promptly, and create opportunities for two-way communication to build relationships and foster brand advocacy.

10. Evolve and Adapt: Continuously monitor market trends, customer preferences, and competitive landscape to evolve and adapt the brand identity over time. Stay agile and responsive to changes in the market and consumer behavior, adjusting brand strategies and tactics as needed to maintain relevance and resonance with the target audience. Embrace innovation and creativity to keep the brand fresh, dynamic, and compelling in the eyes of customers.

Utilizing Digital Marketing Channels

Utilizing digital marketing channels is essential for gun stores and firearms-related businesses to reach and engage with their target audience effectively in today's digital age. Digital marketing offers a wide range of channels and tactics to promote products, build brand awareness, and drive sales online. Here's a detailed overview of utilizing digital marketing channels:

1. Website: A professional and user-friendly website serves as the online hub for the gun store, providing essential information about products, services, store locations, and contact details. The website should be visually appealing, easy to navigate, and optimized for mobile devices to ensure a seamless user experience. Include high-quality images and detailed product descriptions to showcase products effectively. Implement search engine optimization (SEO) techniques to improve the visibility of the website in search engine results and attract organic traffic.

2. Search Engine Marketing (SEM): SEM involves paid advertising on search engines such as Google and Bing to promote the gun store and drive targeted traffic to the website. Utilize pay-per-click (PPC) advertising campaigns to bid on relevant keywords related to firearms, shooting sports, and outdoor activities. Create compelling ad copy and landing pages that align with search intent to maximize click-through rates and conversions. Monitor campaign

performance, analyze key metrics, and adjust bidding strategies to optimize ROI.

3. Search Engine Optimization (SEO): SEO is the process of optimizing the website's content and structure to improve its visibility and ranking in organic search engine results. Conduct keyword research to identify relevant keywords and phrases that potential customers may use to search for firearms-related products and services. Optimize on-page elements such as titles, meta descriptions, headings, and content to incorporate target keywords and improve search engine visibility. Build high-quality backlinks from reputable websites to improve domain authority and enhance search engine rankings.

4. Content Marketing: Content marketing involves creating and distributing valuable and relevant content to attract and engage target audiences. Develop informative and educational content related to firearms, shooting sports, and outdoor activities to address the interests and needs of the target audience. Create blog posts, articles, videos, infographics, and other types of content that provide useful tips, advice, and insights for firearms enthusiasts. Share content on the website, social media platforms, and other digital channels to increase brand visibility and establish thought leadership in the industry.

5. Social Media Marketing: Social media platforms such as Facebook, Instagram, Twitter, and YouTube offer powerful tools for promoting the gun store and engaging with customers. Create and maintain active profiles on relevant social media platforms to share updates, announcements, promotions, and content with followers. Post engaging and visually appealing content such as product photos, videos, customer testimonials, and behind-the-scenes glimpses of the store. Interact with followers, respond to comments and messages promptly, and participate in conversations to build relationships and foster brand loyalty.

6. Email Marketing: Email marketing is an effective channel for nurturing leads, building customer relationships, and driving sales. Build an email subscriber list by offering incentives such as discounts or special offers for subscribing to the email list. Send regular newsletters, product updates, promotions, and personalized offers to keep subscribers informed and engaged. Segment email lists based on customer preferences, purchase history, and demographics to deliver targeted and relevant content that resonates with recipients.

7. Online Advertising: Online advertising platforms such as display advertising, native advertising, and social media advertising offer opportunities to reach target audiences and promote the gun store to a broader audience. Create visually appealing and compelling ads

that highlight products, promotions, and special offers. Target ads based on demographics, interests, and behaviors to reach the most relevant audience segments. Monitor ad performance, analyze key metrics, and adjust ad campaigns as needed to optimize performance and maximize ROI.

8. Video Marketing: Video marketing is an engaging and effective way to showcase products, demonstrate features, and connect with customers on a personal level. Create high-quality videos that showcase firearms, accessories, and related products in action. Produce instructional videos, product reviews, shooting range demonstrations, and customer testimonials to provide valuable information and insights to viewers. Share videos on the website, social media platforms, and video-sharing platforms such as YouTube to increase brand visibility and engagement.

9. Mobile Marketing: Mobile marketing involves optimizing digital marketing efforts for mobile devices to reach consumers on smartphones and tablets. Ensure that the website is mobile-friendly and responsive, with fast loading times and intuitive navigation. Create mobile-friendly content and ad formats that are optimized for smaller screens and touch interactions. Leverage location-based targeting and mobile advertising platforms to reach consumers on-the-go and drive foot traffic to the store.

10. Analytics and Measurement: Utilize digital analytics tools and platforms to track and measure the performance of digital marketing efforts. Monitor key metrics such as website traffic, conversion rates, engagement metrics, email open rates, click-through rates, and social media engagement. Analyze data to gain insights into customer behavior, preferences, and trends. Use data-driven insights to optimize digital marketing strategies, allocate resources effectively, and improve overall performance.

Leveraging Traditional Advertising Methods

Leveraging traditional advertising methods alongside digital marketing can be a valuable strategy for gun stores and firearms-related businesses to reach a broader audience and reinforce brand messaging through various offline channels. Traditional advertising methods offer unique opportunities to engage with potential customers who may not be reached through digital channels alone. Here's a detailed overview of leveraging traditional advertising methods:

1. Print Advertising: Print advertising involves placing advertisements in newspapers, magazines, trade publications, and local publications to reach a targeted audience. Choose publications that cater to firearms enthusiasts, outdoor sports enthusiasts, hunting and shooting communities, and local residents interested in firearms-related topics. Design visually appealing print ads that highlight products, promotions, and special offers. Consider running ads in special editions or seasonal issues related to firearms, hunting seasons, or outdoor activities to maximize relevance and reach.

2. Direct Mail Marketing: Direct mail marketing involves sending physical mail pieces such as postcards, flyers, brochures, and catalogs to targeted mailing lists. Develop eye-catching and informative direct mail materials that showcase products, promotions, and upcoming events. Target specific demographics or geographic areas with a high concentration of potential customers, such as outdoor enthusiasts, hunters, sportsmen, and firearm owners. Personalize direct mail pieces with recipients' names and addresses to increase engagement and response rates.

3. Outdoor Advertising: Outdoor advertising includes billboards, transit ads, posters, and signage displayed in high-traffic areas such as highways, bus stops, train stations, and outdoor venues. Identify strategic locations with high visibility and foot traffic to place outdoor ads that target potential customers driving or commuting in the area. Design attention-grabbing outdoor ads with bold visuals, concise messaging, and clear calls-to-action to capture the attention of passersby and generate interest in visiting the gun store.

4. Radio Advertising: Radio advertising involves airing commercials on local or regional radio stations to reach a captive audience during drive time, commute hours, or specific programming segments. Choose radio stations that cater to demographics interested in firearms, outdoor sports, hunting, and shooting activities. Develop engaging and memorable radio ads that convey key messages, promotions, and offers in a clear and compelling manner. Consider sponsoring radio segments or shows related to firearms, outdoor activities, or hunting to increase brand visibility and association.

5. Television Advertising: Television advertising involves airing commercials on local or cable television networks to reach a broad audience of viewers. Identify television channels or programs that appeal to demographics interested in firearms, outdoor sports, hunting, and shooting activities. Create visually engaging and impactful television ads that showcase products, demonstrate features, and highlight promotions or special events. Consider sponsoring local TV programs, sports broadcasts, or outdoor-themed shows to target specific audience segments effectively.

6. Event Sponsorship and Participation: Sponsorship and participation in relevant events, trade shows, gun shows, and community gatherings provide opportunities to showcase products, engage with customers, and build brand awareness. Identify events that cater to firearms enthusiasts, hunters, sportsmen, and outdoor enthusiasts in the local community or region. Sponsorship opportunities may include logo placement, booth space, product demonstrations, or speaking engagements. Participate actively in events, engage with attendees, and distribute promotional materials such as branded merchandise, brochures, and giveaways to create lasting impressions and connections with potential customers.

7. Local Advertising: Local advertising involves targeting potential customers within the local community through various offline channels such as community newspapers, newsletters, bulletin boards, and flyers. Advertise in local publications, neighborhood newsletters, and community bulletins to reach residents interested in firearms-related topics or outdoor activities. Distribute flyers or door hangers in targeted neighborhoods or outdoor venues frequented by potential customers. Consider sponsoring local sports teams, community events, or charitable organizations to increase brand visibility and support the local community.

8. Public Relations (PR) and Media Relations: Public relations activities involve building relationships with media outlets, journalists, bloggers, and influencers to generate positive publicity and coverage for the gun store. Develop press releases, media kits, and story pitches to pitch to local newspapers, magazines, radio stations, and television networks. Seek opportunities for media coverage, interviews, and feature stories related to the gun store, product launches, special events, or community involvement. Build relationships with local media contacts and influencers to secure favorable coverage and endorsements that enhance brand credibility and visibility.

Hosting Events and Promotions

Hosting events and promotions is an effective strategy for gun stores and firearms-related businesses to attract customers, drive sales, and enhance brand awareness. Events and promotions provide opportunities to engage with customers, showcase products, offer special discounts, and create memorable experiences that encourage repeat visits and build customer loyalty.

Here's a detailed overview of hosting events and promotions:

1. Product Launch Events: Host product launch events to introduce new firearms, accessories, or related products to customers and enthusiasts. Plan a launch event with demonstrations, product showcases, and hands-on experiences for attendees to explore new products and learn about their features and benefits. Offer special discounts or exclusive offers for attendees who make purchases during the event to drive sales and generate excitement.

2. Shooting Range Events: Organize shooting range events or shooting competitions to attract firearms enthusiasts and provide opportunities for hands-on experiences with firearms. Partner with local shooting ranges or outdoor venues to host shooting range

events with target shooting, shooting competitions, or firearm safety demonstrations. Provide expert guidance, safety instruction, and equipment rentals for participants to enjoy a safe and enjoyable shooting experience. Offer promotions or discounts on range fees, equipment rentals, or shooting packages to incentivize participation and drive traffic to the shooting range.

3. Training Workshops and Classes: Offer training workshops, classes, or seminars on firearm safety, marksmanship, self-defense, or concealed carry to educate customers and promote responsible gun ownership. Partner with certified instructors, firearms trainers, or shooting experts to conduct training sessions that cover essential topics such as firearm handling, shooting techniques, legal requirements, and safety best practices. Promote training workshops through email marketing, social media, and in-store signage to attract participants and drive sign-ups.

4. Sales Promotions and Special Offers: Run sales promotions and special offers to incentivize customers to make purchases and drive sales. Offer discounts, rebates, or bundle deals on firearms, accessories, ammunition, or shooting gear to attract price-conscious customers and encourage buying decisions. Create limited-time promotions or seasonal sales events tied to holidays, hunting seasons, or special occasions to create a sense of urgency and drive excitement among customers.

5. Customer Appreciation Events: Host customer appreciation events to thank loyal customers and foster a sense of community among gun store patrons. Organize special events, open houses, or customer appreciation days with complimentary refreshments, giveaways, raffles, or exclusive discounts for attendees. Show appreciation to loyal customers with personalized thank-you notes, special discounts, or loyalty rewards to strengthen relationships and encourage repeat business.

6. VIP Events and Exclusive Previews: Host VIP events or exclusive previews for select customers, industry professionals, or members of loyalty programs to provide exclusive access to new products, services, or promotions. Invite VIP guests to private events with VIP treatment, behind-the-scenes tours, product previews, or exclusive discounts and offers. Build anticipation and excitement among VIP customers by offering early access to limited-edition products, exclusive merchandise, or VIP-only promotions.

7. Holiday and Seasonal Promotions: Capitalize on holidays, special occasions, or seasonal trends to run themed promotions or events that resonate with customers. Plan holiday-themed events, promotions, or sales events tied to major holidays such as Christmas, New Year's, Independence Day, or Thanksgiving. Offer seasonal promotions or discounts on products related to hunting seasons,

outdoor activities, or shooting sports to align with seasonal demand and attract customers seeking seasonal deals.

8. Social Media Contests and Giveaways: Engage customers and generate excitement on social media platforms by hosting contests, giveaways, or sweepstakes with prizes related to firearms, accessories, or shooting gear. Encourage customers to participate in social media contests by sharing photos, videos, or user-generated content related to the gun store or firearms-related topics. Offer prizes such as gift cards, merchandise, or exclusive experiences to winners to incentivize participation and increase social media engagement.

9. In-Store Demonstrations and Vendor Days: Host in-store demonstrations or vendor days with representatives from firearms manufacturers, accessory brands, or industry suppliers to showcase products and provide expert advice to customers. Invite representatives to demonstrate new products, answer customer questions, and offer product recommendations. Collaborate with vendors to offer special discounts, promotions, or giveaways exclusive to the event to incentivize purchases and drive sales.

10. Charity Events and Fundraisers: Organize charity events or fundraisers to support local community organizations, charitable causes, or nonprofit groups while promoting the gun store and engaging customers. Partner with local charities, veterans'

organizations, or community groups to host charity events such as fundraising dinners, charity auctions, or benefit shoots. Donate a portion of event proceeds or sales to the charitable cause and promote the event through marketing channels to raise awareness and encourage participation.

Customer Service and Community Engagement

Customer service and community engagement are critical aspects of running a successful gun store or firearms-related business. These elements are essential for building trust, fostering loyalty, and establishing a positive reputation within the local community and among customers. Here's a detailed overview of customer service and community engagement:

Customer Service:

Providing exceptional customer service is essential for ensuring a positive shopping experience and fostering long-term customer relationships. Gun store owners and staff should prioritize customer satisfaction by offering knowledgeable assistance, personalized recommendations, and attentive support to meet the needs of each customer.

1. Knowledgeable Staff: Employ knowledgeable and trained staff who are passionate about firearms and committed to providing excellent customer service. Staff should be well-versed in product features, specifications, and safety guidelines to offer informed assistance and address customer inquiries effectively.

2. Personalized Recommendations: Take the time to understand each customer's needs, preferences, and skill level to offer personalized product recommendations and solutions. Listen actively to customer questions and concerns, and provide tailored advice and guidance to help customers make informed purchasing decisions.

3. Friendly and Approachable Attitude: Create a welcoming and friendly atmosphere in the store by greeting customers with a smile and offering assistance in a courteous and approachable manner. Encourage staff to engage in friendly conversations with customers, answer questions, and provide assistance without being pushy or aggressive.

4. Prompt Response to Inquiries: Respond promptly to customer inquiries, whether in person, over the phone, or via email or social media channels. Provide accurate and helpful information to address customer questions, resolve issues, and offer assistance in a timely manner.

5. Professionalism and Respect: Maintain a high standard of professionalism and respect in all interactions with customers, regardless of their background or experience level. Treat all customers with courtesy, dignity, and respect, and ensure that staff adhere to professional conduct and ethical standards at all times.

6. Post-Sale Support: Offer post-sale support and assistance to customers to ensure their satisfaction with their purchases. Provide guidance on product usage, maintenance, and safety practices to help customers get the most out of their firearms and accessories. Address any issues or concerns promptly and professionally to ensure a positive resolution.

Community Engagement:

Engaging with the local community is essential for building goodwill, strengthening relationships, and fostering a positive reputation for the gun store. Community engagement initiatives demonstrate the store's commitment to supporting and contributing to the local community while building brand awareness and loyalty.

1. Sponsorship and Support: Sponsor local community events, sports teams, charity fundraisers, or nonprofit organizations to support important causes and initiatives in the community. Consider sponsoring events related to outdoor activities, shooting sports, or

firearms safety education to align with the store's mission and values.

2. Outreach and Education: Offer educational workshops, seminars, or training sessions on firearm safety, marksmanship, self-defense, or concealed carry to educate and empower members of the community. Partner with local law enforcement agencies, shooting ranges, or firearms instructors to provide valuable resources and training opportunities for community members.

3. Community Events and Activities: Host or participate in community events, festivals, or gatherings to connect with residents and promote the gun store within the local community. Set up booths or displays at community events to showcase products, offer demonstrations, and engage with attendees in a fun and interactive way.

4. Volunteerism and Service: Encourage staff and team members to volunteer their time and expertise to support community initiatives, charitable organizations, or local causes. Participate in community service projects, clean-up efforts, or volunteer opportunities to give back to the community and make a positive impact.

5. Open Communication and Collaboration: Maintain open communication channels with community members, local organizations, and stakeholders to stay informed about community

needs and priorities. Collaborate with community leaders, elected officials, and organizations to address issues, support initiatives, and contribute to the overall well-being of the community.

6. Social Responsibility and Advocacy: Demonstrate social responsibility and advocacy by promoting responsible gun ownership, firearm safety, and adherence to legal regulations within the community. Advocate for policies and initiatives that promote firearms safety, education, and responsible use, and engage in constructive dialogue with community members, policymakers, and stakeholders on relevant issues.

Prioritizing customer service excellence and actively engaging with the local community, gun stores and firearms-related businesses can build strong relationships, foster loyalty, and establish a positive reputation that contributes to long-term success and sustainability in the industry.

Building Relationships with Customers

Building relationships with customers is essential for fostering loyalty, repeat business, and positive word-of-mouth referrals for gun stores and firearms-related businesses. Effective relationship-building involves understanding customer needs, providing personalized service, and establishing trust and rapport.

Here's a detailed overview of how gun stores can build relationships with customers:

First and foremost, it's important for gun stores to prioritize customer satisfaction and make every interaction with customers a positive one. This means greeting customers warmly, listening attentively to their needs and preferences, and providing helpful and knowledgeable assistance.

To build rapport with customers, gun stores should strive to create a welcoming and friendly atmosphere in the store. Staff should greet customers with a smile, engage in friendly conversation, and make them feel valued and appreciated. By creating a positive and inviting environment, gun stores can foster a sense of trust and loyalty among customers.

Personalized service is key to building strong relationships with customers. Gun stores should take the time to understand each customer's individual needs, preferences, and budget constraints, and offer personalized recommendations and solutions accordingly. This may involve asking questions to determine the customer's level of experience, intended use for the firearm, and any specific features or requirements they may have.

Consistency is important in building relationships with customers. Gun stores should strive to provide consistent and reliable service to every customer, regardless of the time of day or day of the week. This means maintaining consistent standards of quality, professionalism, and courtesy in all customer interactions.

Communication is crucial for building relationships with customers. Gun stores should stay in touch with customers through various channels, such as email, phone calls, or social media, to keep them informed about new products, promotions, or events. By staying connected with customers and keeping them informed, gun stores can strengthen their relationships and encourage repeat business.

Following up with customers after purchases is an important aspect of relationship-building. Gun stores should follow up with customers to ensure their satisfaction with their purchases, address any post-purchase inquiries or issues, and provide after-sales support as needed. By demonstrating a commitment to customer satisfaction and offering ongoing support, gun stores can build trust and loyalty with customers.

Building relationships with customers requires genuine care and concern for their well-being. Gun stores should go above and beyond to exceed customer expectations and ensure their satisfaction. This may involve going the extra mile to accommodate special requests, providing additional assistance or guidance, or simply being there to listen and offer support when needed.

Handling Customer Concerns and Feedback

Handling customer concerns and feedback is a critical aspect of providing exceptional customer service and maintaining positive relationships with customers for gun stores and firearms-related businesses. By addressing customer concerns promptly, effectively, and empathetically, gun stores can demonstrate their commitment to customer satisfaction and foster trust and loyalty among their customer base. Here's a detailed overview of how gun stores can handle customer concerns and feedback:

Gun stores should prioritize active listening and empathy when addressing customer concerns. When a customer expresses a concern or provides feedback, staff should listen attentively, acknowledge the customer's perspective, and demonstrate empathy and understanding towards their feelings and experiences. By showing empathy and understanding, gun stores can validate the customer's concerns and build rapport with them.

Next, gun stores should respond to customer concerns promptly and professionally. It's essential to address customer concerns in a timely manner to demonstrate a commitment to resolving issues and ensuring customer satisfaction. Staff should acknowledge the customer's concern, offer a sincere apology if necessary, and take proactive steps to address the issue and find a satisfactory resolution.

When addressing customer concerns, gun stores should strive to find a solution that meets the customer's needs and preferences. This may involve offering a refund, exchange, or replacement for defective products, providing additional assistance or guidance, or offering a discount or incentive to compensate for any inconvenience experienced by the customer. By offering a fair and satisfactory resolution, gun stores can demonstrate their dedication to customer satisfaction and build trust and loyalty with customers.

Transparency and honesty are essential when handling customer concerns and feedback. Gun stores should communicate openly and honestly with customers about the steps being taken to address their concerns, any limitations or constraints, and the expected timeline for resolution. Providing clear and transparent communication helps manage customer expectations and build trust and credibility with customers.

Following up with customers after their concerns have been addressed is important to ensure their satisfaction and reinforce positive relationships. Gun stores should follow up with customers to confirm that the issue has been resolved to their satisfaction, address any remaining concerns or questions they may have, and thank them for bringing the matter to their attention. By following up with customers, gun stores can show that they value their feedback and are committed to ensuring their satisfaction.

Gun stores should view customer concerns and feedback as valuable opportunities for improvement. By listening to customer feedback, identifying areas for improvement, and taking proactive steps to address any recurring issues or trends, gun stores can continuously enhance their products, services, and customer experiences. This proactive approach to addressing customer concerns demonstrates a commitment to continuous improvement and customer satisfaction.

Financial Management and Compliance

Financial management and compliance are crucial aspects of running a successful gun store or firearms-related business. Effective financial management involves overseeing the financial activities of the business, including budgeting, accounting, cash flow management, and financial reporting, to ensure financial stability and profitability. Compliance with relevant laws, regulations, and industry standards is essential to ensure legal and ethical business practices and minimize the risk of penalties or fines. Here's a detailed overview of financial management and compliance for gun stores:

Budgeting: Develop a comprehensive budget that outlines projected revenues, expenses, and cash flow for the business. Allocate funds strategically to cover operating expenses, inventory purchases, marketing initiatives, and other business needs while ensuring profitability and financial stability.

Accounting: Maintain accurate and up-to-date financial records, including income statements, balance sheets, and cash flow statements, to track the financial performance of the business. Use accounting software or hire professional accountants to manage bookkeeping tasks, reconcile accounts, and generate financial reports for analysis and decision-making.

Cash Flow Management: Monitor cash flow regularly to ensure adequate liquidity and manage cash flow fluctuations effectively. Implement strategies to optimize cash flow, such as managing inventory levels, negotiating favorable payment terms with suppliers, and controlling operating expenses.

Financial Reporting: Prepare and analyze financial reports regularly to assess the financial health and performance of the business. Review key financial metrics, such as gross margin, net profit margin, inventory turnover, and return on investment, to identify trends, assess profitability, and make informed business decisions.

Tax Compliance: Stay up-to-date with federal, state, and local tax laws and regulations applicable to gun stores and firearms-related businesses. Ensure timely and accurate filing of tax returns, including income taxes, sales taxes, and payroll taxes, to maintain compliance and minimize tax liabilities.

Regulatory Compliance: Comply with all relevant laws, regulations, and industry standards governing the operation of gun stores, including firearm laws, licensing requirements, background check procedures, and record-keeping obligations. Stay informed about changes in regulations and implement policies and procedures to ensure compliance with applicable laws and regulations.

Inventory Management: Implement effective inventory management practices to optimize inventory levels, minimize carrying costs, and maximize inventory turnover. Monitor inventory levels regularly, conduct regular audits, and implement inventory control measures to prevent stock-outs, overstocking, and shrinkage.

Financial Planning: Develop a financial plan that outlines short-term and long-term financial goals, strategies, and projections for the business. Consider factors such as revenue growth targets, expansion plans, capital investment requirements, and financing options to support business growth and sustainability.

Risk Management: Identify and assess potential financial risks and develop risk management strategies to mitigate risks and safeguard the financial health of the business. Consider risks related to market volatility, regulatory changes, legal liabilities, security breaches, and other factors that may impact the financial performance of the business.

Financial Controls: Implement internal controls and procedures to safeguard assets, prevent fraud, and ensure the accuracy and reliability of financial reporting. Establish segregation of duties, authorization processes, and oversight mechanisms to maintain financial integrity and accountability.

Financial Decision-Making: Make informed financial decisions based on thorough analysis, evaluation of risks and opportunities, and alignment with business goals and objectives. Consider factors such as cost-effectiveness, return on investment, and long-term financial sustainability when making financial decisions for the business.

Budgeting and Forecasting

Budgeting and forecasting are essential components of effective financial management for gun stores and firearms-related businesses. Budgeting involves developing a comprehensive plan that outlines projected revenues, expenses, and cash flow for a specific period, while forecasting involves predicting future financial performance based on historical data, market trends, and other factors.

Here's a detailed overview of budgeting and forecasting:

Budgeting:

Budgeting is the process of creating a detailed financial plan that outlines projected revenues, expenses, and cash flow for a specific period, typically on an annual basis. The budget serves as a roadmap for financial decision-making and helps businesses allocate resources effectively to achieve their financial goals and objectives.

To create an effective budget, gun stores should start by identifying their revenue sources, including sales of firearms, ammunition, accessories, and any additional sources such as gunsmithing services or training programs. They should estimate projected sales volumes and prices based on historical data, market trends, and other factors that may impact sales.

Next, gun stores should identify their expenses, including operating expenses such as rent, utilities, payroll, inventory purchases, marketing expenses, and other overhead costs. They should estimate projected expenses based on historical data, industry benchmarks, and anticipated changes in costs or expenses.

Once revenue sources and expenses have been identified, gun stores can create a budget that aligns projected revenues with anticipated expenses while ensuring profitability and financial stability. The budget should include detailed line items for each revenue source and expense category, as well as allowances for contingencies and unexpected expenses. Budgeting also involves monitoring and tracking actual financial performance against the budgeted amounts regularly. Gun stores should compare actual revenues and expenses to the budgeted amounts, identify any variances or deviations, and take corrective actions as needed to ensure that the business remains on track to achieve its financial goals.

Forecasting:

Forecasting involves predicting future financial performance based on historical data, market trends, and other relevant factors. Forecasting helps gun stores anticipate potential changes in revenue, expenses, and cash flow, allowing them to make informed decisions and plan for the future effectively.

To create accurate forecasts, gun stores should analyze historical financial data, including sales trends, expense patterns, and cash flow dynamics. They should also consider external factors that may impact financial performance, such as changes in market conditions, regulatory changes, or economic trends.

Gun stores can use various forecasting techniques, such as trend analysis, regression analysis, and time-series analysis, to predict future financial performance. They should also consider scenario planning and sensitivity analysis to assess the potential impact of different scenarios or variables on financial outcomes.

Forecasting should be an ongoing process that is regularly reviewed and updated to reflect changes in market conditions, business strategies, or other relevant factors. By continuously monitoring and updating their forecasts, gun stores can adapt to changing circumstances and make informed decisions to drive financial performance and business growth.

Budgeting and forecasting are essential tools for gun stores and firearms-related businesses to manage their finances effectively, allocate resources efficiently, and plan for the future strategically. By developing accurate budgets and forecasts, gun stores can make informed financial decisions, anticipate potential challenges or opportunities, and position themselves for long-term success and sustainability in the firearms industry.

Tax Considerations for Gun Stores

Tax considerations for gun stores and firearms-related businesses are important aspects of financial management and compliance. Understanding and adhering to applicable tax laws and regulations are crucial to ensure legal and ethical business practices while minimizing tax liabilities. Here's a detailed overview of tax considerations for gun stores:

1. Federal Taxes:

Gun stores are subject to various federal taxes, including income taxes, payroll taxes, and excise taxes. Income taxes are levied on the net income of the business, which includes revenues from firearm sales, accessories, gunsmithing services, and other sources, minus allowable deductions and expenses. Payroll taxes include Social Security and Medicare taxes withheld from employee wages and matching contributions made by the employer. Additionally, gun stores are subject to federal excise taxes on firearms, ammunition, and accessories under the Internal Revenue Code (IRC) Section 4181.

2. State and Local Taxes:

In addition to federal taxes, gun stores may be subject to state and local taxes, such as sales taxes, income taxes, and business taxes. Sales taxes are typically imposed on retail sales of firearms, ammunition, and accessories to customers within the state. Income taxes are levied on the net income of the business at the state level, while business taxes may include annual license fees or other business-related taxes imposed by local jurisdictions.

3. Sales Tax Compliance:

Gun stores must comply with sales tax laws and regulations in the states where they conduct business. This includes collecting and remitting sales taxes on taxable sales of firearms, ammunition, and accessories to customers. Sales tax rates and regulations vary by state and locality, so gun stores should be aware of the specific requirements in each jurisdiction where they operate.

4. Excise Tax Compliance:

Gun stores are subject to federal excise taxes on firearms, ammunition, and accessories under the IRC Section 4181. The excise tax rates vary depending on the type of firearm or ammunition sold. Gun stores must accurately calculate and collect excise taxes on applicable sales and file excise tax returns with the Internal Revenue Service (IRS) on a regular basis to remain compliant.

5. Record-Keeping Requirements:

Gun stores must maintain accurate and detailed records of their sales, purchases, expenses, and other financial transactions for tax reporting purposes. This includes maintaining sales receipts, invoices, purchase orders, inventory records, payroll records, and other relevant documentation to support tax filings and compliance with tax laws and regulations.

6. Tax Deductions and Credits:

Gun stores may be eligible for various tax deductions and credits that can help reduce their taxable income and lower their overall tax liability. Common deductions and credits available to gun stores may include deductions for business expenses such as rent, utilities, advertising, and employee wages, as well as credits for certain business activities or investments that promote economic development or job creation.

7. Tax Planning and Compliance:

Gun stores should engage in tax planning strategies to optimize their tax position and ensure compliance with applicable tax laws and regulations. This may involve working with tax professionals, such as accountants or tax advisors, to identify tax-saving opportunities, maximize allowable deductions and credits, and develop tax-efficient business structures or strategies.

Tax considerations are important aspects of financial management and compliance for gun stores and firearms-related businesses. By understanding and adhering to applicable tax laws and regulations, maintaining accurate records, and engaging in tax planning strategies, gun stores can minimize tax liabilities, ensure compliance with tax requirements, and contribute to the overall financial health and success of their business.

Ensuring Regulatory Compliance

Ensuring regulatory compliance is a critical aspect of operating a gun store or firearms-related business. Compliance with federal, state, and local regulations is essential to maintain legal operations, uphold public safety standards, and avoid potential penalties or fines.

Here's a detailed overview of ensuring regulatory compliance for gun stores:

1. Federal Regulations:

Gun stores must comply with various federal regulations governing the sale, transfer, and possession of firearms. Key federal regulations include:

- Gun Control Act (GCA) of 1968: The GCA regulates the firearms industry and imposes requirements for firearm sales, licensing, record-keeping, and background checks.

- National Firearms Act (NFA) of 1934: The NFA imposes restrictions on certain types of firearms, such as machine guns, short-barreled rifles, short-barreled shotguns, and suppressors. Gun stores must comply with NFA regulations when selling these restricted firearms, including obtaining the necessary approvals and paying applicable taxes.

- Brady Handgun Violence Prevention Act: The Brady Act requires gun stores to conduct background checks on prospective firearm purchasers through the National Instant Criminal Background Check System (NICS) before completing a sale.

- Bureau of Alcohol, Tobacco, Firearms and Explosives (ATF) Regulations: Gun stores must adhere to regulations issued by the ATF, which oversees federal firearms licensing, inspections, and enforcement activities.

2. State Regulations:

Gun stores must also comply with state-specific regulations governing firearms sales, licensing, background checks, waiting periods, and other requirements. State laws may vary significantly, so it's essential for gun stores to stay informed about the regulations applicable in their operating jurisdictions.

- Some states have additional requirements for firearms dealers, such as mandatory waiting periods, background check procedures, and licensing or registration requirements for firearms purchasers.

- Gun stores must also comply with state laws regarding the sale of firearms to prohibited individuals, such as convicted felons, domestic violence offenders, and individuals with certain mental health conditions.

3. Local Regulations:

Gun stores must comply with local ordinances and regulations imposed by cities, counties, or municipalities where they operate. Local regulations may include zoning requirements, business licensing, signage restrictions, and other specific provisions applicable to firearms-related businesses.

- Gun stores should consult with local authorities or regulatory agencies to ensure compliance with local ordinances and regulations governing their operations.

4. Record-Keeping Requirements:

Gun stores are required to maintain accurate records of firearm transactions, including sales, transfers, acquisitions, and disposals. Federal law mandates specific record-keeping requirements, including the retention of Form 4473 (Firearms Transaction Record) and related documents for a specified period.

- Gun stores must maintain comprehensive records of firearm transactions, including buyer information, firearm descriptions, serial numbers, transaction dates, and other relevant details.

5. Compliance Audits and Inspections:

Gun stores may be subject to compliance audits and inspections conducted by regulatory agencies, such as the ATF or state law enforcement authorities. During inspections, regulatory agencies may review records, inspect inventory, verify compliance with regulations, and ensure adherence to licensing requirements.

- Gun stores should maintain thorough and organized records to facilitate compliance audits and inspections and ensure prompt access to required documents and information.

6. Ongoing Compliance Training:

Gun store staff should receive comprehensive training on federal, state, and local regulations governing firearms sales and transactions. Training should cover topics such as firearm laws, background check procedures, record-keeping requirements, and responsible sales practices to ensure compliance with regulatory requirements.

- Gun stores should provide ongoing compliance training to staff members to keep them informed about regulatory updates, changes in laws, and best practices for maintaining regulatory compliance in daily operations.

Ensuring regulatory compliance is essential for gun stores to operate legally, maintain public safety standards, and uphold their responsibilities as firearms dealers. By staying informed about federal, state, and local regulations, maintaining accurate records, conducting compliance audits, and providing ongoing staff training, gun stores can demonstrate their commitment to regulatory compliance and ensure responsible business practices within the firearms industry.

Future Growth and Expansion

Future growth and expansion are important considerations for gun stores and firearms-related businesses looking to expand their operations, reach new customers, and increase market share. Here's a detailed overview of strategies for future growth and expansion:

1. Market Analysis:

Conduct a thorough market analysis to identify opportunities for growth and expansion in the firearms industry. Evaluate market trends, consumer preferences, competitor analysis, and demographic data to identify target markets, niche segments, and potential areas for expansion.

2. Diversification of Product Offerings:

Consider diversifying product offerings to appeal to a broader customer base and capitalize on emerging market trends. Explore opportunities to expand beyond firearms sales and offer related products and services, such as ammunition, accessories, gunsmithing services, training programs, and shooting ranges.

3. Geographic Expansion:

Explore opportunities to expand into new geographic markets to reach untapped customer segments and increase market penetration. Evaluate potential locations based on demographic factors, market demand, competition analysis, and regulatory considerations to identify viable expansion opportunities.

4. Online Sales and E-Commerce:

Invest in e-commerce capabilities to capitalize on the growing trend of online shopping and reach customers beyond traditional brick-and-mortar locations. Develop a user-friendly website, optimize online product listings, and implement secure online payment processing to facilitate online sales and expand the customer base.

5. Strategic Partnerships and Alliances:

Explore strategic partnerships and alliances with complementary businesses, organizations, or industry stakeholders to leverage resources, expand distribution channels, and access new markets. Collaborate with manufacturers, distributors, shooting ranges, firearms training academies, or outdoor retailers to enhance product offerings and reach a wider audience.

6. Branding and Marketing:

Invest in branding and marketing initiatives to enhance brand visibility, attract new customers, and differentiate the business from competitors. Develop a strong brand identity, implement targeted marketing campaigns, and leverage digital marketing channels, social media platforms, and industry-specific advertising to promote products and services and expand the customer base.

7. Customer Engagement and Loyalty Programs:

Implement customer engagement initiatives and loyalty programs to foster customer loyalty, encourage repeat business, and increase customer lifetime value. Offer incentives such as discounts, rewards, exclusive offers, or membership benefits to reward loyal customers and incentivize repeat purchases.

8. Expansion of Services:

Explore opportunities to expand service offerings to meet the evolving needs of customers and differentiate the business from competitors. Consider offering additional services such as firearm customization, gunsmithing services, firearm training and certification programs, shooting range memberships, or firearm rental services to enhance the customer experience and drive revenue growth.

9. Regulatory Compliance and Risk Management:

Ensure compliance with regulatory requirements and industry standards when planning for growth and expansion. Stay informed about federal, state, and local regulations governing firearms sales, licensing, and operations, and implement robust compliance measures to mitigate risks and ensure legal and ethical business practices.

10. Financial Planning and Investment:

Develop a comprehensive financial plan and investment strategy to support growth and expansion initiatives. Evaluate capital requirements, funding options, and investment priorities to allocate resources effectively and ensure financial sustainability. Consider factors such as inventory management, equipment upgrades, infrastructure improvements, marketing expenses, and staffing needs when budgeting for future growth.

Overall, future growth and expansion require careful planning, strategic decision-making, and a proactive approach to capitalize on opportunities and overcome challenges in the firearms industry. By exploring diverse growth strategies, investing in branding and marketing, enhancing customer engagement, and ensuring regulatory compliance, gun stores can position themselves for long-term success and sustainable growth in the evolving marketplace.

Assessing Opportunities for Growth

Assessing opportunities for growth is a critical step for gun stores and firearms-related businesses looking to expand their operations, reach new customers, and increase market share. This process involves evaluating various factors, including market trends, consumer preferences, competitive landscape, and internal capabilities, to identify potential growth opportunities and develop strategic plans for future expansion.

One approach to assessing opportunities for growth is conducting a comprehensive market analysis. This involves analyzing market trends, industry reports, and consumer behavior to identify emerging opportunities and niche segments within the firearms industry. By understanding market dynamics and customer preferences, gun stores can identify areas of unmet demand or underserved customer needs that present opportunities for growth.

Competitive analysis is another important aspect of assessing opportunities for growth. By evaluating competitors' strengths, weaknesses, market positioning, and strategies, gun stores can identify gaps in the market and competitive advantages that can be leveraged to differentiate their offerings and capture market share. This may involve analyzing competitors' product offerings, pricing strategies, marketing tactics, and customer service practices to identify areas for improvement and differentiation.

Assessing internal capabilities and resources is also essential when evaluating opportunities for growth. Gun stores should evaluate their current infrastructure, operational efficiency, staffing capabilities, and financial resources to determine their readiness for expansion. This may involve conducting a SWOT (strengths, weaknesses, opportunities, threats) analysis to identify internal strengths that can be leveraged, weaknesses that need to be addressed, and opportunities for growth that align with the organization's capabilities.

In addition to market analysis and internal assessment, gun stores can also explore partnerships and collaborations as a strategy for growth. This may involve forming strategic alliances with manufacturers, distributors, shooting ranges, or other industry stakeholders to expand distribution channels, access new markets, and enhance product offerings. Collaborating with complementary businesses or organizations can also provide opportunities to cross-promote products, share resources, and reach a broader customer base.

Assessing opportunities for growth requires a proactive approach to innovation and adaptation. Gun stores should continuously monitor market trends, consumer preferences, and regulatory changes to identify new opportunities and adapt their strategies accordingly. This may involve investing in research and development to innovate product offerings, exploring new sales channels such as e-commerce or mobile apps, or expanding into adjacent markets or product categories to diversify revenue streams.

Assessing opportunities for growth requires a holistic approach that considers market dynamics, competitive landscape, internal capabilities, and external factors. By conducting thorough market analysis, evaluating internal resources, exploring strategic partnerships, and embracing innovation, gun stores can identify and capitalize on opportunities for sustainable growth and long-term success in the firearms industry.

Expanding Product Offerings

Expanding product offerings is a strategic growth initiative that gun stores and firearms-related businesses can pursue to diversify revenue streams, attract new customers, and capitalize on emerging market trends. This process involves identifying complementary products and services that align with the core business while meeting the evolving needs and preferences of customers.

Here's a detailed overview of expanding product offerings:

1. Market Research:

Begin by conducting thorough market research to identify trends, consumer preferences, and potential gaps in the market that could be addressed through expanded product offerings. Analyze industry reports, customer feedback, and competitor analysis to gain insights into emerging opportunities and areas of unmet demand within the firearms industry.

2. Customer Needs Analysis:

Understand the needs and preferences of your target customers by soliciting feedback, conducting surveys, and analyzing purchasing patterns. Identify complementary products and services that align with the interests and purchasing behaviors of your customer base, ensuring that new offerings add value and enhance the overall customer experience.

3. Product Selection:

Select product categories or services that complement your existing offerings and appeal to your target market. Consider expanding into related categories such as hunting gear, outdoor accessories, shooting apparel, safety equipment, firearm maintenance supplies, or training programs. Evaluate potential suppliers and product quality to ensure that new offerings meet the standards expected by your customers.

4. Strategic Partnerships:

Explore partnerships with reputable manufacturers, distributors, or suppliers to expand your product offerings effectively. Collaborate with trusted brands or industry leaders to access a wider range of products, negotiate favorable pricing terms, and enhance the credibility of your offerings. Consider exclusive partnerships or co-branded initiatives to differentiate your product lineup and create a competitive advantage.

5. Product Merchandising and Display:

Optimize store layout and product merchandising to showcase new offerings effectively and attract customer attention. Create dedicated sections or displays for expanded product categories, featuring eye-catching signage, product demonstrations, and promotional materials to highlight key features and benefits. Consider cross-merchandising strategies to encourage add-on purchases and increase sales.

6. Staff Training:

Provide comprehensive training to staff members to educate them about new product offerings, features, and benefits. Equip staff with product knowledge, sales techniques, and customer service skills to effectively communicate with customers, address inquiries, and drive sales of expanded product categories. Encourage staff to upsell or cross-sell complementary products and services to enhance the overall shopping experience.

7. Marketing and Promotion:

Develop targeted marketing campaigns and promotional initiatives to introduce new product offerings to customers and generate excitement. Utilize various marketing channels such as social media, email marketing, in-store signage, and advertising to create awareness and generate interest in expanded product categories. Offer special promotions, discounts, or incentives to encourage trial purchases and stimulate sales.

8. Customer Feedback and Adaptation:

Solicit feedback from customers regarding new product offerings to gather insights into their preferences, satisfaction levels, and purchase behavior. Monitor sales performance, customer feedback, and market trends to assess the success of expanded product categories and make adjustments as needed. Adapt product offerings based on customer preferences, market demand, and competitive dynamics to optimize sales and profitability.

9. Continued Evaluation and Iteration:

Continuously evaluate the performance of expanded product offerings and iterate on strategies to maximize sales and customer satisfaction. Monitor key performance indicators such as sales growth, profit margins, inventory turnover, and customer feedback to assess the effectiveness of new product categories. Adjust pricing, merchandising strategies, and promotional tactics based on real-time data and market feedback to optimize results.

Expanding product offerings requires careful planning, market research, strategic partnerships, and effective execution to successfully introduce new products and services that resonate with customers and drive business growth. By identifying complementary offerings, leveraging strategic partnerships, and executing targeted marketing initiatives, gun stores can diversify their product lineup and create additional revenue streams while enhancing the overall customer experience.

Scaling Operations

Scaling operations is a strategic process that involves expanding the capacity and capabilities of a gun store or firearms-related business to accommodate growth, increase efficiency, and meet the demands of a growing customer base. Scaling operations requires careful planning, investment in resources, and implementation of scalable processes and systems to support business expansion while maintaining quality and profitability.

At the core of scaling operations is the need to increase production capacity, streamline processes, and improve operational efficiency to accommodate growing demand. This may involve expanding physical infrastructure, investing in technology and automation, optimizing supply chain management, and enhancing workforce productivity to meet increased sales volume and customer demand.

Expanding physical infrastructure may include acquiring additional retail space, opening new store locations, or investing in warehouse and distribution facilities to accommodate growing inventory and support expanded operations. This requires careful site selection, facility design, and construction management to ensure that new facilities meet the needs of the business and provide a seamless customer experience.

Investing in technology and automation can help streamline operations, improve productivity, and reduce labor costs associated with scaling operations. This may involve implementing inventory management systems, point-of-sale (POS) systems, e-commerce platforms, and customer relationship management (CRM) software to automate processes, improve data visibility, and enhance customer engagement.

Optimizing supply chain management is essential for scaling operations effectively. This may involve sourcing products from multiple suppliers, negotiating favorable pricing terms, and implementing efficient inventory management practices to ensure adequate stock levels and minimize stock-outs. Establishing strong relationships with suppliers, optimizing procurement processes, and implementing just-in-time inventory practices can help minimize carrying costs and improve inventory turnover.

Enhancing workforce productivity is crucial for scaling operations while maintaining quality and customer service standards. This may involve hiring additional staff, providing comprehensive training programs, and implementing performance management systems to support employee development and maximize efficiency. Cross-training employees, establishing clear roles and responsibilities, and fostering a culture of continuous improvement can help optimize workforce productivity and adaptability.

In addition to physical infrastructure, technology, supply chain management, and workforce productivity, scaling operations requires a focus on maintaining quality, customer service excellence, and brand reputation. Implementing quality control measures, monitoring customer feedback, and investing in customer service training can help ensure that business expansion does not compromise product quality or customer satisfaction.

Scaling operations requires a strategic approach that considers various aspects of the business, including physical infrastructure, technology, supply chain management, workforce productivity, and quality assurance. By investing in resources, implementing scalable processes and systems, and maintaining a focus on quality and customer service excellence, gun stores can effectively scale their operations to accommodate growth and achieve long-term success in the firearms industry.

Planning for Long-Term Success

Planning for long-term success is crucial for gun stores and firearms-related businesses to sustain growth, adapt to market changes, and thrive in a competitive industry. Long-term success requires strategic planning, continuous innovation, and a proactive approach to addressing challenges and opportunities.

Here's a detailed overview of key considerations for planning long-term success:

1. Vision and Mission:

Establish a clear vision and mission statement that outlines the long-term goals, values, and purpose of the business. Define the desired outcomes and aspirations for the business and articulate how it aims to serve customers, contribute to the community, and differentiate itself in the marketplace.

2. Strategic Planning:

Develop a comprehensive strategic plan that outlines the business's objectives, strategies, and action plans for achieving long-term success. Conduct a SWOT analysis to identify strengths, weaknesses, opportunities, and threats, and use this analysis to inform strategic priorities, resource allocation, and decision-making.

3. Market Analysis:

Conduct ongoing market analysis to monitor industry trends, consumer preferences, and competitive dynamics. Stay abreast of emerging technologies, regulatory changes, and market shifts that may impact the firearms industry. Continuously assess market opportunities and threats to inform strategic decisions and adapt business strategies accordingly.

4. Innovation and Adaptation:

Embrace innovation and adaptability as key drivers of long-term success. Invest in research and development to innovate product offerings, improve operational efficiency, and differentiate the business from competitors. Stay agile and responsive to changing customer needs, market trends, and technological advancements to remain competitive and relevant.

5. Customer Focus:

Maintain a customer-centric approach by prioritizing customer satisfaction, loyalty, and retention. Listen to customer feedback, gather insights through surveys and feedback mechanisms, and use this information to enhance products, services, and overall customer experience. Build strong relationships with customers based on trust, transparency, and personalized service to foster long-term loyalty and advocacy.

6. Talent Development:

Invest in talent development and employee engagement to build a high-performing team that is aligned with the business's long-term goals and values. Provide opportunities for professional growth, training, and skill development to empower employees and foster a culture of continuous improvement and innovation. Recognize and reward top performers to motivate and retain talent over the long term.

7. Financial Management:

Implement sound financial management practices to ensure long-term financial stability and sustainability. Develop realistic financial projections, monitor key performance indicators, and track financial performance against strategic goals. Maintain a strong focus on cost management, cash flow optimization, and risk mitigation to weather economic fluctuations and achieve long-term profitability.

8. Brand Building and Reputation Management:

Invest in brand building and reputation management to establish a strong and reputable presence in the marketplace. Build brand awareness through targeted marketing, consistent messaging, and positive customer experiences. Monitor online reputation, address customer concerns promptly, and uphold ethical business practices to safeguard and enhance the business's reputation over the long term.

9. Community Engagement and Corporate Social Responsibility:

Demonstrate commitment to corporate social responsibility (CSR) and community engagement initiatives to build trust and goodwill with customers, employees, and stakeholders. Support local communities through philanthropic efforts, sponsorships, and partnerships with charitable organizations. Align CSR initiatives with the business's values and priorities to make a positive impact while enhancing the brand's reputation and long-term success.

10. Continuous Improvement:

Embrace a culture of continuous improvement and learning to drive long-term success. Encourage feedback, foster collaboration, and empower employees to contribute ideas and initiatives for innovation and process improvement. Regularly review and evaluate business strategies, performance metrics, and market trends to identify opportunities for optimization and adaptation to ensure sustained growth and competitiveness.

Conclusion

In conclusion, establishing and operating a successful gun store or firearms-related business requires careful planning, strategic decision-making, and a commitment to excellence in every aspect of operations. Throughout this guide, we have explored various key components essential for building and sustaining a thriving business in the firearms industry.

From understanding the historical context and regulations governing firearms to navigating compliance requirements, licensing, and permits, it's evident that regulatory adherence and responsible gun ownership are fundamental pillars of the business. Moreover, fostering a culture of safety, education, and responsible gun ownership not only enhances customer trust but also contributes to the overall well-being of the community.

Expanding product offerings, scaling operations, and planning for long-term success are crucial strategies for driving growth and maintaining a competitive edge in the market. By diversifying product lines, optimizing operations, and embracing innovation, gun stores can adapt to changing market dynamics and meet the evolving needs of their customers while ensuring long-term sustainability and success.

Furthermore, prioritizing customer service, community engagement, and brand reputation is essential for building strong relationships with customers and stakeholders, fostering loyalty, and enhancing the overall customer experience. By investing in employee training, talent development, and corporate social responsibility initiatives, gun stores can create a positive impact in their communities while building a reputable brand known for its integrity and commitment to excellence.

In conclusion, success in the firearms industry requires a holistic approach that encompasses regulatory compliance, customer satisfaction, operational efficiency, and long-term strategic planning. By prioritizing these key components and continuously striving for excellence, gun stores can position themselves for sustained growth, resilience, and success in the dynamic and competitive firearms market.

RECAP of key points.

Throughout this guide, we've covered a wide range of essential topics for opening and operating a successful gun store.

Let's recap the key points:

1. Understanding the Firearms Industry: We explored the historical context and evolution of firearms, as well as the current landscape of the firearms industry.

2. Regulations and Compliance: Gun stores must adhere to federal, state, and local regulations governing firearms sales, licensing, record-keeping, and safety. Compliance with regulations ensures legal operations and promotes responsible gun ownership.

3. Licensing and Permits: Obtaining the necessary federal firearms license (FFL) and complying with state-specific licensing requirements are crucial for operating a gun store legally.

4. Market Research and Business Planning: Conducting thorough market research, analyzing competitors, and developing a comprehensive business plan are essential steps for launching and growing a successful gun store.

5. Financial Management: Effective financial management, including budgeting, forecasting, and managing finances, is essential for long-term success and sustainability.

6. Customer Service and Community Engagement: Prioritizing exceptional customer service, building relationships with customers, and engaging with the local community are key to fostering loyalty and enhancing the overall customer experience.

7. Product Offerings and Inventory Management: Diversifying product offerings, implementing effective inventory management systems, and sourcing reliable suppliers are crucial for meeting customer needs and maximizing sales.

8. Marketing and Promotions: Developing a strong brand identity, implementing targeted marketing strategies, and leveraging digital and traditional advertising channels are essential for attracting customers and driving sales.

9. Scaling Operations and Planning for Long-Term Success: Planning for growth, scaling operations, and implementing strategies for long-term success involve careful strategic planning, investment in resources, and a focus on innovation and adaptation.

10. Compliance and Responsible Gun Ownership: Gun stores play a vital role in promoting safety, education, and responsible gun ownership by complying with regulations, providing training and educational resources, and fostering a culture of safety.

By focusing on these key points and implementing best practices in each area, gun store owners can establish and grow successful businesses while promoting responsible gun ownership and contributing positively to their communities.

Final Words of Advice

As you embark on the journey of opening and operating a gun store, I'd like to offer some final words of advice:

1. Prioritize Safety and Compliance: Safety should always be your top priority. Ensure that your store complies with all federal, state, and local regulations governing firearms sales, licensing, and safety measures. Invest in training for yourself and your staff to promote responsible gun ownership and safe handling practices.

2. Build Trust and Relationships: Building trust with your customers and community is essential for long-term success. Focus on providing exceptional customer service, fostering open communication, and demonstrating integrity in all your interactions. Building strong relationships with customers and stakeholders will set your store apart and contribute to your reputation as a trustworthy business.

3. Stay Informed and Adapt: The firearms industry is dynamic and constantly evolving. Stay informed about changes in regulations, market trends, and customer preferences. Be willing to adapt your business strategies and offerings to meet the evolving needs of your customers and stay ahead of the competition.

4. Invest in Training and Development: Invest in training and development for yourself and your staff to ensure that you have the knowledge and skills necessary to run a successful gun store. Stay up-to-date on industry best practices, attend relevant workshops and seminars, and seek opportunities for continuous learning and improvement.

5. Engage with the Community: Engage with your local community and establish your store as a trusted and respected member of the community. Participate in community events, support local charities and organizations, and be an active participant in local initiatives. Building strong ties with the community will not only attract customers but also contribute to the overall success and sustainability of your business.

6. Seek Support and Guidance: Don't hesitate to seek support and guidance from industry associations, fellow gun store owners, and other professionals in the firearms industry. Networking with others in the industry can provide valuable insights, advice, and support as you navigate the challenges and opportunities of running a gun store.

Opening and operating a gun store is a significant undertaking, but with careful planning, dedication, and a commitment to excellence, you can build a successful and rewarding business that promotes responsible gun ownership and serves the needs of your customers and community.

Wishing you the best of luck on your journey!

A. Glossary of Key Terms:

1. Federal Firearms License (FFL): A license issued by the Bureau of Alcohol, Tobacco, Firearms, and Explosives (ATF) that allows individuals or entities to engage in the business of manufacturing, importing, or dealing in firearms.

2. National Firearms Act (NFA): A federal law regulating the sale and transfer of certain firearms and accessories, including machine guns, short-barreled rifles/shotguns, suppressors, and destructive devices.

3. Compliance: The act of adhering to laws, regulations, and standards governing the firearms industry, including federal, state, and local regulations related to firearms sales, licensing, and safety measures.

4. Inventory Management: The process of overseeing and controlling the flow of inventory, including tracking stock levels, managing replenishment, and optimizing inventory turnover to ensure adequate stock levels and minimize stock-outs.

5. Customer Relationship Management (CRM): A technology-driven strategy for managing interactions and relationships with customers, including storing customer information, tracking interactions, and analyzing customer data to enhance customer satisfaction and loyalty.

B. Sample Forms and Templates:

1. Firearms Purchase Form: A form used to document the sale of firearms to customers, including customer information, firearm details, background check information, and sales transaction details.

2. Firearm Transfer Record (Form 4473): A form required by federal law for firearm transactions conducted by licensed firearms dealers, including information about the purchaser and details of the firearm being transferred.

3. Firearm Acquisition and Disposition Record (ATF Form 4473): A form used by federal firearms licensees (FFLs) to record the acquisition and disposition of firearms in their inventory, including information about the firearm, acquisition details, and purchaser information.

4. Employee Training Log: A template used to track employee training and development activities, including training topics, dates, attendance, and training outcomes.

5. Inventory Replenishment Template: A template used to forecast inventory needs and manage inventory replenishment, including tracking inventory levels, reorder points, and lead times for replenishment.

C. Additional Resources and References:

1. Bureau of Alcohol, Tobacco, Firearms, and Explosives (ATF): The federal agency responsible for enforcing firearms laws and regulations in the United States. The ATF website provides resources and guidance on federal firearms laws, regulations, and compliance requirements.

2. National Shooting Sports Foundation (NSSF): The trade association for the firearms industry, providing resources, education, and advocacy for firearms retailers, manufacturers, and enthusiasts.

3. Gun Store Owner Forums and Communities: Online forums and communities for gun store owners, providing opportunities for networking, sharing best practices, and seeking advice from fellow industry professionals.

4. Firearms Industry Publications: Publications such as Gun Digest, Shooting Illustrated, and Recoil Magazine provide industry news, product reviews, and insights for firearms retailers and enthusiasts.

5. Local, State, and Federal Government Websites: Websites for local, state, and federal government agencies provide information on firearms laws, regulations, and licensing requirements specific to your location.

These resources can serve as valuable tools and references for gun store owners and firearms-related businesses seeking to navigate the complexities of the firearms industry and operate their businesses successfully and responsibly.

www.ingramcontent.com/pod-product-compliance
Lightning Source LLC
Chambersburg PA
CBHW071917210526
45479CB00002B/453